Praises for Refined by Fire:

Patricia Juster's *Refined by Fire* delivers what it promises. Patty allows us into her private chamber with the Lord, where she walks through the dark times with him only to come up repeatedly with precious and unexpected treasures. Many fellow travelers will find refreshment here as they walk through their own dark night of the soul.

—*Don Finto, pastor emeritus, Belmont Churches, author of Your People Shall Be My People*

Patty Juster has found a place near the heart of God that few ever find. Patty has walked through many valleys of the shadow but has turned each one into a wellspring of life. The insights into the ways of God that Patty gives us in this book are invaluable treasures.

—*Steve Fry, recording artist and speaker*

Patty Juster writes not from the protective courts of the theological chambers of conceptual ideas but from the depths of her own personal experiences and struggles. Her spiritual journey is a living proclamation that the God of the Scriptures is good and faithful. Patty is not afraid to ask the hard questions because in her pain and pursuit she has discovered one who ever bids us to come closer and to dig deeper into the mystery of his dealings and of the wonder of his ways.

—*Dottie Schmitt, founding pastor, Immanuel's Church, Silver Spring, Maryland*

Refined by Fire

PATRICIA JUSTER

Refined by Fire

A Grieving Mother
Finds Treasures Hidden in Darkness

TATE PUBLISHING & Enterprises

Published by Tate Publishing & Enterprises, LLC
127 E. Trade Center Terrace | Mustang, Oklahoma 73064 USA
1.888.361.9473 | www.tatepublishing.com

Tate Publishing is committed to excellence in the publishing industry. The company reflects the philosophy established by the founders, based on Psalm 68:11,
"The Lord gave the word and great was the company of those who published it."

Book design copyright © 2010 by Tate Publishing, LLC. All rights reserved.
Cover design by Scott Parrish
Interior design by Joel Uber

Published in the United States of America

ISBN: 978-1-61663-955-6
1. Biography & Autobiography / Personal Memoirs
2. Religion / Christian Life / Death, Grief, Bereavement
10.09.09

Dedication

Firstly, I would like to dedicate this book to my Lord and Messiah, who is my life. He has been my comforter and teacher and has never left me. He has been faithful to bring me through each valley and reveal a little more of himself each time. May he gain glory through the testimony shared here, for he is the treasure hidden often in darkness.

Secondly, I would like to dedicate this book to my beloved son, Samuel Peter, whose life has enriched me from earth for over twelve years and now is enriching my life from heaven. May the meaning of the calling of his life be fulfilled and the prophetic voice and evangelism be restored to Israel.

Also, I would like to dedicate this book to my precious mother, whose godly example and prayers were an anchor to me through both the good times and bad.

I would be remiss if I did not include here a thank you to Capt. Walter Stottlemeyer, Jr. for risking his life to rescue our son and the other boys from the fiery inferno. He sustained second and third degree burns as the house flashed over. This book is also dedicated to the many firefighters who serve the community every day, not taking their own lives into account.

Lastly, I would like to dedicate this book to my best friend, my husband. Dan's faith in me has enabled me to come to this place where I could write a book. His kindness, integrity, and love of truth have continued to nurture me through almost forty years of marriage! How I love him and am grateful for the four wonderful children he gave me. Benjamin, Rebecca, and Simcha have become pure gold as they have endured patiently the trials with us and have embraced God as their refuge and strength.

Table of Contents

Foreword

Are you hungry for deeper fellowship with God? When I finished reading the final chapter of this wonderful book, I knew my savior better. I could not help but love God more. There is an almost unbearable agony, beauty, and intimacy revealed in these pages. Few books I have read contain such treasures. This is the story of a true prophetess like Elizabeth in the New Testament. Patty and her husband, Dan, have been at the forefront of the restoration of Jewish life and community in the Messiah. Like all pioneers, they have lived dramatically; in so doing they have given to the world a story more gripping than fiction and more instructive than the wisest thesis. Rarely have I read a book that is so disarmingly honest. Patty invites us to explore her inner life. Through unspeakable tragedy and sorrow, we sink with her into dark depths only to be ambushed by her testimony of supernatural comfort, peace, and restoration. Our deepest fears begin to melt as we comprehend the riches of divine love. Because Patty is so completely open and vulnerable, we are able to receive her teaching about the truly hard questions surrounding suffering and the character of God. Her words become an expression of the heart of God to us, like ointment or salve for the wounds of life.

Maturity is defined by the degree to which we have come out of deception into truth concerning ourselves. God knows us perfectly, but do we see ourselves as he sees us? Do we have his perspective on our story? This is what strikes me about this book. Patty knows her own story, the story of God dealing with her, testing her, shaping her. She has not allowed her treasure to trickle through her fingers and be lost. The riches of the years are all there, and you and I are invited in to benefit by them.

This is a book for the mountain as well as the valley; there is more here than healing and comfort for broken hearts. Here we find an excellent guide to the use of the gifts of the spirit and an exploration of the subject of divine healing. Above all else, this is a magnificent treatise on the character of God. Patty's life teaches us that the privilege always outweighs the price when it comes to knowing God and doing his will.

—John Dawson
Founder, International Reconciliation Coalition
President, Youth With a Mission

PART ONE

Experiencing
Light and Darkness

Some sat in darkness and the deepest gloom, prisoners suffering in iron chains ... he brought them out of darkness and the deepest gloom and broke away their chains. Let them give thanks to the LORD for his unfailing love and his wonderful deeds for men, for he breaks down gates of bronze and cuts through bars of iron.

Psalm 107:10, 14–16

Valley Shadows

Even though I walk through the valley of the shadow of death, I will fear no evil, for you are with me; your rod and your staff... comfort me.

Psalm 23:4

"Fire! Fire!"

Dan and I rushed downstairs in response to the alarming call. Out our front door I bounded, immediately turning left toward the house where Sam, our youngest child, was sleeping. Mud oozed through my bare toes as I almost slipped down the slope between our houses...

Almost a year had passed since that fire. How very different was that June evening of 1998 from the day in April 1999. Dan and I were traveling in Israel on a prayer journey to intercede at important sites related to early Christianity and the first Messianic Jews. In the Judean Desert where we were, millions of rocks and scorched, burnt-orange dirt covered the hillsides. There was no mud and no fire, only a few Israeli cacti scattered along the desert landscape. How appropriate it seemed to begin writing this book from that location.

I remember the tour guide explained that it is in the desert where one finds God. In fact, David wrote many of his psalms in this very same desert. The guide went on to say that one might wonder where shepherds grazed their sheep since it was so dry. It was in the valleys, he said, where water collects for the shepherd to feed his sheep, not at the mountaintops as one might suppose. Yes, God does feed us in the valley where things may seem barren and dark. It is there where we truly begin to know God.

I next remember heading toward the lowest point on Earth, which is almost four hundred meters below sea level. This place bordered on the Dead Sea, reminding me that not long ago I reached my lowest point on my personal journey. Even God's face seemed hidden from me then. My life bordered on a similarly lifeless sea. Sleep was far from me. During the day I wished it were night, and at night I wished it were day. Terror gripped me on every side. Darkness disturbed my rest and clouded my soul. Even decisions were difficult for me; deciding which of two apples was in better shape almost sent me into a panic. Most horrifying of all, my normal ability to read the Bible and to pray evaded me. My emotions and body were out of control too. Doctors gave it a name: Post Traumatic Stress Disorder, PTSD.

That made sense. After all, in June of 1998, our youngest child, Samuel Peter, died from injuries he received in that house fire. Part of my soul seemed ripped from me, and my life was set on a whirlwind course following his death. While attempting to cope with the intensity of my grief—with this darkness of soul—my back went out. I was in constant pain. Doctors said it was caused by a degenerative disk disease and there was nothing they could do. Such agony of grief and physical pain proved unbearable.

As if that wasn't enough, I began to experience heart palpitations. A cardiologist discovered that my heart valve was deteriorating and he believed my heart was regurgitating eighty percent of its blood; in other words, my heart may only be pumping at twenty percent capacity. So, in December of 1998, I went through a difficult procedure to assess the extent of heart valve damage. I woke up in the middle of the test with a big black tube stuck down my throat. The doctors were using this tube to take echoes of my heart through my stomach. I wasn't supposed to regain consciousness during the procedure. The good news was that my heart was only regurgitating forty percent of its blood. The bad news was that I would not be able to have a valve repair, only a replacement, and they didn't want to fix it until I couldn't stand the symptoms of being out of breath any longer. (A few years after this was written I did go for heart valve surgery, and they were able to repair my valve instead of replacing it!)

Within a couple of days, I was called to be with my dying mother, to help with her nursing care until she passed away. Pancreatic cancer had emaciated her to such an extent that she was only a shell of her usual robust self. I couldn't handle any more stress; I was off the chart!

Life came to a halt as I traversed through what appeared to be a barren desert. I could no longer change my circumstances by my will and dint of effort. My back and heart limited my physical activity; my emotions robbed me of peace and of my ability to cope. I could no longer do what I wanted to do. I found myself in utter darkness where no one could reach me, though many good-hearted friends certainly tried. My only answer was God; only he could deliver me. So it was in the desert that he had me … I was alone in a dark, desolate place with him.

In the months following, however, I began to discover certain treasures that could only be found in the darkness. As I was plunged deeper and deeper into death of self and the loss of so much I held dear, I came to an unfathomable understanding of the power of resurrection life found in Jesus through the Holy Spirit. Although I despaired of life itself, God was faithful. He breathed new life into me as many all over the world prayed vigilantly for me, my husband, and my entire family. I honestly can say that I was once dead but now I am alive. That barren place from which I began this writing became the place where I found the treasure of resurrection life and the glory of a faith refined in fire.

As you read about the events of my life, you will find my grief process was a journey of rediscovering the treasure of life itself. Emerging from the darkness was a pattern of life for me—trial, hardship, grief, pain, doubt, and fear were conquered by love, faith, trust, and then life and light.

Although most of this book was written during the second year after Samuel's death, I hope you see I have found the gold refined in fire and a joy no one can take away. This is the story of how I obtained my pearl of great price: the knowledge of the preciousness of Jesus's life living in me, the hope of glory. This simple truth became my reason for living. I was placed on this earth to do his will, and the scripture concerning the one who has suffered much, that he "does not live the rest of his earthly life for evil human desires, but rather for the will of God" (1 Peter 4:2) took on roots. As you read my story, may you find encouragement for the trials you may be facing at this time. There is a hope and a future for you as you allow life's challenges to chip away at all other motivations but the one ... to please God.

Youthful Radiance

For you have been my hope, O Sovereign LORD, my confidence
since my youth. From birth I have relied on you; you brought me
forth from my mother's womb. I will ever praise you.

Psalm 71:5–6

I do not think it would be fair if I wrote about these tragic events without first providing some of the history of my life with God; the trials and tests I recently went through did not happen in a vacuum. God prepared me over a lifetime for that horrible day on June 14, 1998, and for the years that followed. God never leads us into situations beyond what we are able to handle. It is through a lifetime of trials, difficulties, temptations, and valleys that I was strengthened to take on the bigger battles.

I am reminded of when the Israelites first left Egypt. God did not call upon them to go through the land of the Philistines, which was a shorter route. There they would have had to face war, but they were not yet ready. Even David faced the lion and the bear before he had to fight Goliath. Like them, I was not allowed to take the shortcut. Because of my past history, I was confident God would once again bring me through victoriously. With that said, here is my journey.

My precious mother, Jane, married my father in 1946 when she was twenty-one. She had a homespun beauty that spoke of English strength and gentleness. Her nose was delicately formed; she had dark brown hair and soft, kind, brown eyes. My father, Homer, thought Jane was gorgeous and did not waste much time before marrying her.

Homer had met my mother on a blind date while he was on leave from the army, as he had just completed a tour in the Philippines during World War II. He was a dark-haired man of medium height with a barrel chest. Both of my parents had serious, sedate temperaments because each had suffered greatly during different seasons in their life.

My father's mother died shortly after childbirth, and his father ran away, leaving him in the care of his grandparents. My mother's family also broke apart, but it was in her young adulthood when her father abandoned her mother for another woman. Several times during her childhood, her father came home drunk and became abusive to the family. And so, these two from broken families were thus joined.

Within a year after my parent's marriage, she gave birth to my sister, Pam. Before Pam was two months old, my mother became pregnant again. In March of 1949, she gave birth to my brother, David.

What a challenge it was to care for two babies and to adjust to a new marriage. It appeared to be too much for her. In fact, three months later when she found herself pregnant with me, she was shocked. So, in her dismay, she attempted to do things that might cause her to miscarry naturally. She lifted heavy weights and ran up and down stairs, but all to no avail. I was there to stay even though the spirit of death was already at work to take my life before I was born. (My mom has since deeply repented to God and to me, and sometimes we were even able to have a good laugh about it. Even though my siblings would disagree with me, I was later her favorite child. She praised God for preserving my life, and I became a blessing to her and not a curse.) Life had triumphed over death!

From my earliest memories, I can recall standing on the pews of the church and singing the old Baptist hymns at the top of my lungs as I hung onto my father's arm. He couldn't sing on key, but that was okay because I couldn't either. Nevertheless, I remember having a very tender heart toward the things of God at an early age.

It is a mystery why God chose to give me a tender heart. Perhaps all children are born with this. Maybe it comes from being blessed with such a godly heritage. As far back as we can trace our family tree on my mother's side, there have been believers and several full-time missionaries or ministers. It reminds me of the scripture where Paul says of Timothy, "I have been reminded of your sincere faith, which first lived in your grandmother Lois and in your mother Eunice and, I am persuaded, now lives in you also" (2 Timothy 1:5).

Yes, my mind can still see my dear mother kneeling and praying before her "quiet time chair." She would regularly get up at 5:30 a.m. to spend time with the LORD. I also know my godly grandmother faithfully prayed for me day and night. And then there was my missionary aunt and uncle who would come home on furlough and share such amazing accounts of God's faithfulness on the mission field. The fervor each of these had for the LORD became pressed into my young, impressionable spirit. I have such a rich heritage!

And so it should be no surprise to you when I say I can never remember a time when I did not love Jesus or a time when he wasn't my best friend. However, I do remember a specific time, around the age of four, when I had a supernatural encounter with God as I was playing with my older brother and sister.

As I recall, we had dug a pit in our vegetable garden in the back of our house. We lived on our small farm in Pennsylvania, and we were taking turns playing Joseph, throwing each other into the hole. As we were playing, I felt the favor of God shining upon me. I looked up to the sky and saw the rays of the sun coming through some dark clouds, and they appeared to form a cross. Worship entered my spirit, and the LORD captured my heart. But it wasn't until I turned five years of age that I officially gave my heart to him.

Even at that young age, I knew I was a sinner and needed forgiveness. I can never forget the warmth of the sun that day and the joy I felt as I sat with my Sunday school teacher on a huge boulder overlooking New York's Hudson River. It was there that I gave my life to Jesus and felt the Holy Spirit enter my heart. There was no doubt; I was God's child. I readily shared my faith with my friends and anyone who would listen.

Later, when I was almost seven, we moved to another city in New York. While going to a small Baptist church some distance from our house, I came to love the Word of God and to worship in a deep way. I was fed from the richness of God's Word for about ten years by a pastor who loved God with all his heart. Later in my life, I discovered the pastor was born Jewish but gave up this identity to become a devout Baptist minister. I will always be grateful for his impartation into my own life.

I gained a love for the nations too while at that small Baptist church. Every so often a missionary came through and fascinated me with the stories of God's faithfulness and the joy of winning the lost to the LORD. Then, after speaking, they would call people forward who felt the Holy Spirit prompting them to dedicate their lives to that particular country the missionary represented. I came forward and committed my life to so many different countries; I couldn't imagine how God was ever going to straighten it out. I knew from an early age I was to serve God in some full-time capacity. At fourteen, I was convinced I heard God call me to be a missionary nurse somewhere in Africa.

God's mercy enabled me to respond to his love. However, my sensitive heart was both a blessing and a challenge. It was a challenge because everything became magnified, whether good or bad. I remember weeping as a child when I played the song "I'd Rather Have Jesus Than Silver or Gold" on my little record player. I played this song over and over again. Then, of course, there were the times I would cry about the poor children in different parts of the world who were not born to believing parents. I prayed for the children behind the iron curtain because I thought it was a literal thing hanging from the sky. I would become sincerely emotional, all because of how sensitive I was to the things of God.

In high school, I carried my Bible to school and was not quiet about my faith. But because of my openness with others, it wasn't long before I began to experience rejection. A lot of times I ate lunch alone. I did not know how to fit into the crowd and suffered greatly during these teen years. Many times, I would be ridiculed and excluded from the friendships of my classmates. I remember one time in history class when all the guys turned around in their chairs and stared at me. They called me "fat Pat" even though I wasn't fat; they did this just because it rhymed and they knew it bothered me. I was devastated. Years later, I found out that I annoyed them by my nervous laugh, and they just wanted to be mean. But God had his purpose, and it was during these years of pain and rejection that I began to learn to press into God as my refuge and strength. I was having regular times with him every day and grew in intimacy with him. Unfortunately, I did not know how to transfer his love to my classmates. I reasoned that all I needed was God and thought, *Who cares about their friendship?* After all, I really did not "need" them. I had my life at church. In an attempt to shield my heart from further pain coming from rejection, I convinced myself that I could be self-sufficient.

It was at church that I came alive. I went to almost every service in the little Baptist church in upstate New York: Sunday morning, Sunday night, youth group, and the Wednesday night prayer meeting. If I had a ride, I was there. Punishment to me was being forced to stay home. Additionally, whenever the pastor asked for testimonies, I had to stand up and find something to praise God about. I loved to proclaim his Word and couldn't seem to keep quiet. One time my pastor laughed and shook his head. He said, "Pat, someday you are going to be a preacher." Those who knew me laughed with my pastor. What he said was true. It seems I can't cease from proclaiming God's goodness, and I still do so today with even more of a sense of urgency and conviction, because I sense the needs for encouragement are so great. The world seems to be in a state of crisis; many are fearful.

My life up to this point was pretty uneventful as you can see. There were just the usual things children go through: broken bones, tonsillectomy, cuts, and emotional bruises. I lived a pretty sheltered life. Often, I would be ashamed of my testimony because I did not believe it was very exciting. I never did drugs, got too involved with guys, drank, partied, or committed any of the other common teenage rebellions. I was a goody-goody. Yet, the last Sunday evening before going off to college, somehow I knew life would never be the same. The following poem serves as a foreshadowing of what was to come.

Not My Will
Against the door frame of my heart
I stood my soul. Its heights I marked
So small it was—so very small
I thought if God could see at all
He'd understand it could not bear
Much suffering, or pain or care
But, though I knew that in God's eyes
I must appear of minute size;
Deaf to my pleas for leniency,
He heaped great burdens upon me;
And my poor soul was forced to bear
What seemed so much more than its share
But, though it flinched and fluttered anew
Somehow (God must have known) it grew
Each burden brought new strength, new heights
I often think how well it might be small,
And weak and helpless still—
If God had yielded to my will.

—Anonymous

Cloudy College Days

My purpose is that they may be encouraged in heart and united in love, so that they may have the full riches of complete understanding, in order that they may know the mystery of God, namely, Christ, in whom are hidden all the treasures of wisdom and knowledge.

Colossians 2:2–3

My college days were tumultuous. I entered Wheaton College during the late sixties, when the country was going through an upheaval of ideology and a war that did not have the heart-and-soul backing of Americans. Youths were becoming disillusioned with the American dream. The climate of the country seeped into the college campuses—or perhaps it was the other way around. Not even Christian colleges could escape these powerful forces unleashed against the young at that time. Many became skeptics at Wheaton; however, this was not the fault of the college. The philosophy courses were taught with great conviction, whereas I felt the Bible courses and my integration of Christian thought into the various areas of study were weak. There was a growing group of students who were dissatisfied. Perhaps the atmosphere at the college just reflected the times in which we found ourselves.

Like many other students, I was not equipped with an adequate knowledge of spiritual warfare to combat the strong spiritual forces working to divide two generations. Parents coming out of the Great Depression had sought to give their children all the material goods they were denied. They raised their children on Dr. Spock's philosophy of parenting. As a result, I believe, a generation grew up that was greatly indulged and undisciplined for the most part. Two working parents began to be the norm, and the children started to feel alienated. A rift between two generations enlarged; the youth did not want to receive the wisdom from their elders any longer. Although these phenomena could be applied to every generation, I think that the sixties were unique to American history. The young people were rebelling against materialism, a meaningless war, and all authority. They no longer wanted the empty way of life handed down to them. They were looking for something more to devote their lives to. Many students dropped out of our colleges at that time and became hippies in search of the "better life." (Interestingly enough, in the midst of this darkness, God birthed the Jesus Movement. Many young people came to faith at this time. In fact, most of the older Messianic Jewish leaders in America and Israel are former hippies who came to faith during the Jesus Movement revivals.)

It was in this context that I was shaken out of my sheltered upbringing. Suddenly, it seemed my simple faith began to become very complicated. Too much introspection began to erode my faith, and a flood of questions overwhelmed me—questions such as: how can I be sure there is a God? How can God love so many people? How can a good God allow so much evil to continue? Why doesn't he answer when I call upon him? Why do I have to keep up my daily discipline of quiet time? Can't I find God on my own terms? Do I believe what I believe because of what my parents taught me or because it is really true?

I was desperate for answers and did not realize the destructive power of unfettered, relentless doubt. Also, I did not understand the spiritual warfare necessary to break through the darkness that was clouding out the light. Many times it was too hard for me, so I gave up the fight of faith and accepted a worldview without God.

During this time, I met my future husband, Dan, who was a professional skeptic. He came to Wheaton College for his junior year, having transferred from King's College in New York. While attending King's, he had a nervous breakdown and was still suffering from the aftereffects of unbelief and fear. He too came from a fundamentalist background, and when his understanding of the end times was challenged at King's, he discovered that Scripture really did not back up what he was taught. He reasoned that if this belief was wrong, which was taught so forcefully by the teachers at the summer camp he had attended, how could he be sure of the other tenets of faith he had been taught? One morning while at King's, he woke up to a devastating hollowness and deep anxiety. He thought he no longer believed in God or Jesus or even the Bible as God's revelation. As he tried to read Isaiah, the voices in his head kept saying, "This is a myth. This is not believable; this is made up by man." As at Wheaton, the enemy of our souls was working overtime to plant seeds of doubt in our hearts and those of students at King's College.

There were several factors leading up to that terrible morning, yet Dan hadn't noticed the warning signs. In short, his breakdown resulted from zealous burnout in his Christian service and the breaking off of a relationship with a disturbed young woman. He moved to Wheaton to get a fresh start and become a philosophy major; Wheaton had some of the best professors in this area of study. How shattered his life had become in contrast to the zealous teenager who had fire in his bones. He felt called to ministry and did not even see why it was necessary to go to college, but going to college and seminary was the accepted practice of training.

Dan became hungry to know the truth. The loss of faith was so painful for him that he forced himself to read everything he could get his hands on that might answer his questions. In fact, he kept a card file of all his questions, and, as he received answers to each question, he recorded them on the appropriate card. He drove his professors nuts with all his questions. It took a long time for all his questions to be answered, but, even then he did not come back to a living faith. His skepticism lasted almost four years. He found that the pursuit of truth was not just a pursuit of knowledge through the intellect, but a revelatory pursuit with his spirit and the Holy Spirit.

Dan and I grew close as we spent hours together talking about our faith struggles. I think we became each other's sounding board and our hearts were knit together as a result. Through our pain of skepticism we fleshed out our common values. We were united in a shared quest to find God and were committed to return to the place of joy we once knew. So there we were, two troubled people who found each other in their misery. If it were not for the living example of Jesus in one man, Evan Welsh—then the chaplain of Wheaton College—we probably would have dropped out and become hippies too. The words of scholars could not penetrate our confused hearts, only the love of God coming through this one man's life could (along with the love of his wife, Olena Mae). Excerpts from the journal I kept should show you just where I was at that time. Those powers of skepticism and cynicism were very strong back then, and both Dan and I almost did not come out of our despair.

21 *January '69*

I lay here in bed wondering who I am and where I am going. Is there a God? I cannot deny his existence because I believed in him all my life. Without God there is nothing—with him I have real purpose and life. If God is there, then he is so powerful and wonderful that he transcends all understanding. God is really here despite what I believe, so why not believe? I want to serve God with all my life—my life is his. How long do I wait? Is my faith based on emotion? But how can I be sure of my faith without emotion? Can I believe in God just by reason alone? Oh, just to be his child, his obedient child.

1 *March '69*

I must be patient and wait. God has started a good work in me and I shouldn't be discouraged when the going is rough. He is making me go through this period of doubting so that I will be able to understand and help others going through this same thing. In my generation, the major issue is not "which denomination is right" but "whether or not there is a God." I have to know what to say to an atheist, so I must get an education and experience the doubts of atheists. No matter how much I doubt, though, way down deep I believe there is a personal and loving God. I praise God for molding me and making me into his child. We are made for his glory, and it is only through giving him glory that we can feel like a whole person.

2 *March '69*

I pray but there is no answer. I ask, and I do not receive. I seek, and I do not find. God promises strength and help for the day, but I cannot find it. They say that you shouldn't plead and whine to God for something. You are supposed to praise him. So I praise him. I praise him so hard that I get pains in my soul. Does he hear? I get discouraged because it is like praying to air. How can I know he is there when I do not hear him? I have done just what the Bible has said: repent, be baptized, and be filled with the Holy Spirit. Where is that abundant life he has promised? Maybe I am too far gone—a reject—yet he has used others worse than me. I ask not for miracles; all I ask is what he promises his children they can have. Maybe I am living in an illusion. Oh, that God might hear me and save me from this doubt and temptation.

As you can see by my entries, what was being challenged was the basic biblical truth that those who seek God must believe he exists and that he rewards those who seek him (Hebrews 11:6).

One time I became so desperate that I lay facedown on the floor in our dorm prayer room and pounded the floor. I was asking God that if he was there, why didn't he reveal himself to me. After many tears, I looked outside the window to see if there was any sign in the sky, but alas, there was none. I needed evidence that he existed and that he cared enough about me to speak to me. The following journal entry illustrates just where I was then.

21 *April '69*

I wish life would slow down long enough so that I can find myself. Who am I? Life is loaded with deadlines, tests, and papers. Have to earn money, be friendly, and do what I am told. Don't wear shorts or stay out too late. Clothes cost money and so does food. Studying costs money in order to earn money. Reality is made up of molecules, so they say, non-extended. I am nothing. Why do I exist? They say to worship someone up there whom no one has ever seen or heard. Oh yes, people claim that the Bible says he is there all right, but why doesn't he talk to me? I pray—how absurd—to a nothingness almost. How many people are enough before he has enough to worship him? I feel like a chess piece moving about in life from square to square, one year to the next. All life is like a game. If we are put here to worship, then how come all the extra doings of life, work, school, sleep, eat, and drink? Seems like each is put through as much as he can stand (or not stand) down here. Some never find out why. I suffer in order to be a better person, but why must I be better? They say I'm free. We all must die because we all were born—how is that free, I ask you? I feel like God is up there with a club hitting me down every time I feel good and saying, "Go back and learn your lesson." What lesson? If he wants to tell me something why doesn't he come out and say so instead of beating around the bush? Oh well, perhaps my destiny is to be mediocre, never rising above "blahness." Yes, this world is too funny; you neither can be too happy nor too sad. People are unreal most of the time. Do they know who they are and why they are here? There is only one road to travel for happiness and peace, but all ways have misery. I guess the choice is up to personal preference—misery for purpose or misery for misery's sake.

My philosophy of life at that time was to expect the worst so I would not get disappointed. This was my poor state, and all I could do was write in an endeavor to address it. During the sixties, that was what people did when they were depressed; they talked about it, sang about it, wrote about it, and smoked weed to deal with it (though I never did that, thank God.)

The times of breaking through to God were rare, yet even during this season he was teaching me compassion and endurance. He was there all along. Even though I may have seemed faithless, he remained faithful. What a powerful truth to learn—an anchor in times of doubt and darkness. I think the truth about the steadfast character of God was the greatest treasure I procured from this season. The following journal entry records one of those precious times of light shining through the darkness.

9 May '69

A strange quietness has overcome me, as if I have come up for a breath of air. I have been under a long time, seeking fearfully for what I was afraid was not there. I can remember other times when such a feeling has overcome me. It is like the sun breaking through the clouds during a storm for a brief moment, just to let us know that it is still there. When my troubles lessen (when God is made known to me) then life seems worth living again. Perhaps God, like the sun, shows himself to me after I have been through a storm to reassure me there is nothing to fear, that he is still there. Perhaps he is like a rope pulling me up just when it feels like I am drowning. I haven't drowned yet; he always brings me up for air. I think he is keeping me down longer and longer, though, to get me used to life as it really is, to face the real issues and to get the right answers. Perhaps it is my job to help others find the rope of life before they drown or point them to the "sun" of God. It is nice to know God is here.

You can see the beginning of some revelation of God breaking through. Remember when Isaiah saw the LORD? It was the year that King Uzziah died. He saw him high and lifted up, sitting upon a throne. All he could do was fall on his face and worship. Out of darkness came such glory! It was true for me back then and is still true today. Whenever we are going through those dark valleys, there is the joy of discovering the knowledge of the glory of God in the face of Yeshua. I found this development in three journal entries that came within four days of each other.

23 October '70

I can't stand it; I need somebody to love so badly. I want some-one to care for and give myself to. Maybe that someone is God. My heart is torn. I want love, and I can't find it—yet I am scared to find it. I want someone to hold me in his arms and tell me everything is okay and not to worry. I want to feel the love of warm lips upon my tear-stained cheeks; oh why doesn't someone care? But someone does care; God cares. He loves me and wants the best for me. Why doesn't God take me in his arms? What part of me is unwilling to give into God? Oh, I want God to rule my life. What must I do? Why doesn't he answer? I love him so and in him I know I will find love, but when? I can't stand living in loneliness anymore. I have to have a purpose. Oh LORD, help me. Where are you? Save me from this unhappiness! I am starving, God, feed me.

25 October '70

Life is confusing; I don't know what I want in life. Who am I? Where do I fit in? Everything seems so unreal; where are real people? People seem so fake; I am fake. Do I really exist? Oh, God, I wonder about so many things: infinity, life, love, people, and places. Where do things fit in? Why the suffering in the cities? Why doesn't God do something? There is no human hope for lost people in the cities. There are so many people who are doomed. I love people, and I want to understand them down deep, but sometimes I cannot communicate. Oh LORD, this world lacks love ... unselfish love.

Then, for some reason, as the next entry reveals, I experienced a respite in the midst of the darkness. The sun broke through the clouds, and I felt warmed by God's presence. When I saw him, I saw my uncleanness, and then I wanted to serve him—just like when Isaiah saw the LORD.

26 October '70

Oh, Jesus, thank you for everything. I don't deserve all that you have done for me. I have complained and bickered about my problems; they are so puny compared with others. You are so patient with me. How can I thank you? I want you to rule my life. You make me so happy. I want to get to know people and love them. LORD, free me to love. LORD, prepare me for your service. Mold me and make me into the kind of person you want me to be. Show me and teach me, LORD. Oh, how I love Jesus!

Oh, the wonder of discovery. One preacher so beautifully described what the responses of the living creatures surrounding the throne of God might be like. He said that perhaps the living creatures continually cry, "Holy, holy, holy is the LORD Almighty," because their eyes are always on his glory, and every time he moves, a different aspect of his character in its greatness is revealed. The power of that revelation evokes another response of worship. You almost cannot help yourself.

My journey out of darkness was not a straight line. Sometimes, it was two steps forward and three steps back. But in the end God's light shone through the darkness, and there were longer periods without the clouds hiding the light.

Darkest Night

You hem me in—behind and before; you have laid your hand upon me. Such knowledge is too wonderful for me, too lofty for me to attain. Where can I go from your spirit? Where can I flee from your presence? If I go up to the heavens, you are there; if I make my bed in the depths, you are there. If I rise on the wings of the dawn, if I settle on the far side of the sea, even there your hand will guide me, your right hand will hold me fast. If I say, "Surely the darkness will hide me and the light become night around me," even the darkness will not be dark to you; the night will shine like the day.

Psalm 139:5–12

During the summer of '69 the foundations of my life—which were already weakened—blew apart into a thousand different pieces. I wonder now how anyone could have survived what I went through. It was hard enough in college facing such forces of darkness arrayed against us young people. We were not prepared. Perhaps the only people praying for me were my mother; grandmother; my chaplain, Evan Welsh; and his wife. But no matter how dark it became, there was yet a light inside of me that refused to go out.

God's grace sustained Dan and me, even though much of the time we did not feel it. An anchor deep within my heart held me secure in the midst of the storms and kept my ship from drifting too far away. Sometimes, I think about how close I came to missing my calling. I would have been miserable if I had not ended up in full-time ministry. Oh, the love that would not let us go. How we could have so easily fallen into gross sin, but his love held us tight and kept us safe. Even though I went through the valley of the shadow of death that summer, and even though it felt like all hell broke loose, God was in control.

The following journal entry was dated five days before the valley experience that forever changed my life. A powerful spirit of fear was attacking me. It very well could have been a forewarning.

3 August '69

It has been a long time since I have written in this journal and things are no better—in fact, they are worse. My fears of the unknown have increased. Each night brings new nightmares. I have to check the closets and the floors underneath the bed for unwanted visitors every night before turning in. It is a fear of being strangled and clubbed—night is when one is most helpless—especially me, because I sleep on my left ear and am almost deaf in the other. Sounds go unheard, sounds that may save my life. There is no reason for me to be afraid. My reason tells me that no one will harm me for I live way out in the country. Besides, we have a dog and plenty of people in the house. Yet my reason goes unheard. My reason tells me there is a God, but if there is, why hasn't he cleaned up my mess yet? I've tried everything: repentance, baptism (twice even), acceptance of the Savior and the Holy Spirit. I went through all the rituals of being a Christian. I even had those good feelings, but they are all gone now. I think too much. At night I clutch my body and try to gain the essence of its being. I look at the walls of my room and the ceiling. I look outside and then inside me. How absurd living is! There seems to be more questions than answers, more people dying in their own misery than people living in the answer. Life is but an ordeal that will soon pass. Nothing lasts. Broadcasts announce crime after crime, muggings, riots, rapes, robberies, and scandals. When will it stop? Life is getting worse, not better. Everybody is suffering… I am in a stupor. I don't know where to turn. I know what I want, but he doesn't listen. Every night I cry for him. Where can I find him? When will he listen? My insides are decaying, my nerves are wearing out. How much longer? I can't go on playing the Christian game. They say what to do, but it doesn't work; I've tried it. I keep on saying maybe someday I'll find it. Words fail me; I can't put off my night's ordeal any longer, but when and how will I find life?

Just five days later, my brother, David, and my best friend, Karen, started out on a picnic to the local falls. I went to work as usual for my father in his data processing business. His business was one of the first computer-operated billing systems. At that time in history it took two rooms to contain the computers, which cost thousands of dollars to rent. The old relics all had to be programmed through wiring the master boards by hand. Each year, they had to be changed and updated because the computer technology was changing so rapidly.

I was the keypuncher. My job was to enter billing information from a particular business's records, using a kind of typewriter that punched holes into small cardboard cards. These cards would then be fed into a computer that would read the holes and perform certain functions. On this particular afternoon in August, I was sitting at my desk punching holes in cards when a policeman came to the office.

8 August '69

Well death has struck home. David is dead. He was twenty years, not yet a man, not yet placed in this world. I was working in the office when a cop walked in—they always seem to bring bad news. When he went outside with my father, I told everyone in a loud voice that cops bring trouble. Dad came in as white as a sheet. As he grabbed hold of my arm to steady himself he said, "Dave is dead." I got hysterical. Why, why me? Why us? No, it can't be true, but it is; I must face it. I must be strong for my parents. It is harder on them. It is funny, but when death strikes, people enter into a state of unreality. People to call, arrangements to be made, tears to be shed. Dad called our pastor, Bo, and Uncle Ramsey. A friend had to drive us home. Death brings a multitude of acts done in vanity. Vanity, vanity, all is vanity. Children had to leave the house so that Dad could tell Mom. Then the kids found out. I must be brave, but who am I kidding? My head aches. Dave is in heaven, I believe. Karen is bad off. There will be scars, deep scars that will remain unhealed. Dave, poor Dave; he wasn't straightened out yet even. He still had questions to be answered. They say we should thank God, for we will see fruit being reaped from this. The TV is going— anything to forget—but we can't. He is dead. I am thinking of him now and wondering if he suffered. I wish he would tell God how hard Mom is taking it. She thinks it is her fault because she didn't say her prayers for him that morning. But if we were to put the blame on anyone it could be on mankind. It is funny, but I am not bitter, just confused and scared. I was the last one to see

David and Karen. They were on their way to a picnic when they ran into a cement truck. David is a careful driver; it cannot be his fault. I love David, but God loves him more.

How can I even describe the weight of grief, shock, and disbelief I went through when David died? The first few weeks I was quite numb. Experts on the grieving process say hormones kick in as a kind of anesthesia, and this enables a person to appear very heroic. Not long after the funeral, my emotions erupted as the initial shock wore off. The reality of his death set in, and feelings that spanned the whole spectrum—anger, fear, rage, jealousy, disbelief, blame, depression, and guilt—rushed in. I experienced them all. It felt surreal, as if I had had a stroke and could not get my body to do what my brain told it to do.

Tears were hard to release. How proud we were of David for having finished his first year at the Air Force Academy with honors. He had such a bright future. I was plagued with questions about the meaning of his death. I wondered how God would ever get glory out of it. Furthermore, we wanted to know why he had to die and whether or not there would be fruit coming from the tragedy. I was already looking for some sign of life coming from his death that would give it purpose. I pondered whether a price tag could be placed on his death to make it all worth it. We later found out that several young men did come to faith as a result of David's witness and death.

There were no grief counselors to help walk us through my brother's death, and each member of the family had to work through his grief alone. For example, while riding in the limo on the way back from the funeral, my father said, "Stop that crying." That sent a strong signal that all grieving had to be done in private; we were not allowed to cry together. Little did we know that this one event would alienate our family emotionally for over thirty years. Instead of the pain of loss bringing us together, we were forced to suffer alone in silence. We all walked around masking our grief, pretending all was well. We thought our feelings were not valid or appropriate and even felt ashamed of those feelings.

A week after David died, Karen died from her injuries, too. I was in a daze. My favorite sibling was dead, and now my best friend was dead too. She was on life support for a week before she died. During that week, there was much prayer that went up for her healing. Some "crazy charismatics"—as I called them then— even went so far as to broadcast over the radio that she would be healed. But when she died, they had to put the blame elsewhere in order to save face, so they said there must have been some sin in her life that prevented her from being healed. Of course this enraged me and was a factor that hindered me for several years from opening up more to the Holy Spirit. Their words felt like they were coming from one of Job's comforters; instead of bringing healing and hope, they were like vinegar on an open wound. Today, I look back on this lack of sensitivity on the part of these Christian radio personalities as immaturity and not a matter of intentionally trying to cause more pain. As I have watched myself in difficult situations, I have even found myself inadvertently speaking words that bring pain instead of comfort. It is not easy to say the right thing to a hurting person, and sometimes it is best to just not say anything.

As we all continued to deal privately with our grief, my mom went around the house in a daze, guilt-ridden for not having prayed for David in the morning. She longed to join David in heaven. Her pain was so great that heaven, at this season of her life, appeared to be her only hope of freedom. That, however, left us children feeling like we did not matter, that we were not enough of a reason for Mom to want to live. I did not understand that, in the midst of the intense pain of grief, all other affections were diminished in the face of the one that was lost.

Then there was the isolation we felt from our friends at church who did not know how to act around us. And my parents' friends seemed to ignore us as they attempted to bring my parents comfort. I felt left out, as if what I felt did not count compared to their suffering. Little regard was given to the fact that he was our brother. Inside, I was crying out to be noticed. I wondered if my parents were even aware that we hurt too. There was nowhere to turn for comfort.

A month after these tragic deaths, my sister and I returned to Chicago. I returned to Wheaton, and Pam went back to be with her new husband. Shortly after beginning the new school year, my freshman roommate died of a complication resulting from surgery. And then on the heels of this news, I received word that my grandfather had died. Death surrounded me. I was thrown into a violent grief. No one seemed to understand. I wept almost every day, it seemed, and I alienated many of my friends. My heart cried, "Where are you, God?" It was as if I had stood back and was looking at the devastation following the wake of a tornado. Debris from demolished houses and lives seemed to encompass the horizon of my future. All sense of security in God's care seemed shattered. And yet I had nowhere else I could turn.

I found that intense pain can isolate a person more than any other factor. Severe loneliness accompanied me when I returned to Wheaton College. At that time, only one person could enter into my suffering sufficient enough to bring comfort, the chaplain of Wheaton College, Evan Welsh. Because he had lost his first wife in a car accident and had suffered deeply through other trials, he had the capacity to sit and listen with great compassion. Tears would roll down his cheeks as he heard me recount the pain of my loss again and again. This brought comfort in that I no longer felt as lost and alone.

Once again, the circumstances of my life put me in a position where God was the only way out. Everywhere I turned, there was only pain. I drew upon my childhood knowledge of God and slowly began to press into him. I had to find him. It was life or death. But, somehow, I knew he was in ultimate control and he loved me. This belief held me like an anchor, and the simple faith of a child's song especially brought comfort. "Jesus loves me, this I know, for the Bible tells me so. Little ones to him belong; they are weak but he is strong."

Dan's ongoing encouragement kept me in college during the months following this tragedy. Even though we were not married until July of 1971, our commitment to each other provided a much-needed fortress. We clung to each other, and combining what little strength we each had empowered us to go on.

I also drew comfort from the following scripture, although I felt like my "tree" was cut down to the ground: "But as the terebinth and oak leave stumps when they are cut down, so the holy seed will be the stump in the land" (Isaiah 6:13). As Israel was restored to her land and began to prosper again, so I too had hope that one day I would grow back and bear fruit once again. Though it appeared that death had gotten the victory, there was a resurrection just around the corner.

My precious readers, I want you to know his love would not let me go—to know the keeping power of his spirit is stronger than death. No matter how many times you might stumble and fall, no matter how dark it might get, you also have this hope of the resurrection that keeps you secure. The following song brought me solace; may it comfort you, as well.

O love that will not let me go,
I rest my weary soul in Thee;
I give Thee back the life I owe,
That in thine ocean depths its flow
May richer, fuller be.

O Cross that lifted up my head,
I dare not ask to fly from thee;
I lay in dust life's glory dead,
And from the ground there blossoms red
Life that shall endless be.
Matheson and Peace, 1984

This intense grief went on for six months until one afternoon when I was taking a nap in my college dorm room. There, I had a vision of Jesus and my brother in the room with me. They came over to me with such love on their faces and took hold of my hand and said, "Enough of mourning, get on with living." Something lifted from me, and a healing and comfort was put in its place. I don't know how this fits into your theology, but I do know that I was broken and then I was put back together. From that time on, I did not grieve. I felt sadness at times, but there was no longer any heaviness or intense pain.

Though it looked like death triumphed, life took hold of me. I consider it a miracle from God that I survived and even was able to continue my studies. Dan was a great support at this time. He would not let me drop out, no matter how much I pleaded with him.

Flickering Faith

Your kingdom is an everlasting kingdom, and your dominion endures through all generations. The LORD is faithful to all his promises and loving toward all he has made. The LORD upholds all those who fall and lifts up all who are bowed down.

Psalm 145:13–14

This healing, however, did not take care of the other issues of my life. During the weeks ahead, I continued to try to draw strength from God and rebuild my shattered faith. On the weekends, Dan would come in from Trinity Evangelical Divinity School. (He went there to study philosophy of religion after graduating from Wheaton.) He would cut down all my arguments for believing. I found out later that he was afraid I would become some spiritual giant and dump him. It wasn't too many months, however, before God soundly rebuked him for doing this to me.

Dan was traveling down a dark country road on his way back to seminary when God said to him, "You hypocrite! How can you continue to destroy Patty's faith with arguments that you have already answered? You know the truth. It is up to you to make the choice to believe again." This scared him so much and brought him under such conviction that he called me to apologize as soon as he got back to his room.

We were a sight to behold. Many said we were bad for each other but not Chaplain Welsh. He believed in us and said we were perfect for each other—and thank God for his faith!

Through that year and the next, our faith was gradually strengthened. As Dan was studying the Gospels with an open heart, he came to the place where Jesus asked Peter, "Who do you say I am?" and Peter responded, "You are the Messiah, the Son of God." At that point Dan broke down and cried. He had found the truth! In less than a year after Dan's faith transformation we were married.

I did not know it at the time, but because of all the traumas of my freshman summer and the fall of my sophomore year, I began to display different manifestations of fear. Today, it could be diagnosed as Post Traumatic Stress Disorder (PTSD). I wish I had known it back then because I suffered silently. I began to develop different phobias that carried over into my marriage: fear of open spaces, fear of choking, fear of my breathing stopping, and just plain fear of death. Plus, our early marriage years were very stressful as two self-centered, traumatized individuals (Dan recovering from depression, and I from the many losses in my life) learned to love each other. There were fireworks many an evening.

We were very immature, but God did not look on the outward appearances. He delighted in taking the weak and foolish things of our lives to confound the wise. We qualified on every account of being unqualified. But, by the strange workings of God, Dan and I ended up pastoring a small Presbyterian church in Chicago as soon as I finished college in 1972. We had been married only a year. He needed this student intern assignment to finish up his seminary degree from McCormick Theological Seminary. God had done such a work in Dan's life that, after studying about every major religion, he concluded the only true religion was the Judeo-Christian faith. No other religion or worldview even came close to being as consistent, cohesive, or comprehensive.

Dan pursued his original calling as a pastor, and we ended up in the Presbyterian Church because of the influence of our dear chaplain and spiritual father, Evan Welsh, who was Presbyterian. The church he was filling in for as interim pastor just happened to be called the First Hebrew Christian Presbyterian Church. Chaplain Welsh put two and two together (Dan's Jewish heritage and his Presbyterian ordination) and knew this was the perfect place for his intern assignment. Dan was only twenty-four, and I was only twenty-two when we took up this pulpit.

Before I met Dan, I had not even known that Jews still existed. On TV on the weekends, they would encourage the listeners to go to their synagogue or church to worship. I thought that *synagogue* was another name for church. (Now I have found myself among people who have been resurrected from the dead—these Jewish believers. Up until this time in history, it was considered to be unscriptural to identify oneself as both a Jew and a Christian.

When a Jew came to faith, he had to give up all his Jewish identity.)
All that Dan and I wanted was a small Presbyterian church in the
country where we could preach the gospel. We did not ask for
this pioneer work among the Jews, but God had different ideas.
So began my lifelong call of identification with the Jewish people
who soon became my people. Jesus then became Yeshua to me,
and life for me as a Christian drastically changed.

A Brilliant Branch

In that day the branch of the LORD will be beautiful and glorious, and the fruit of the land will be the pride and glory of the survivors in Israel.

Isaiah 4:2

In days to come Jacob will take root, Israel will bud and blossom and fill all the world with fruit.

Isaiah 27:6

As I said, Dan and I never planned on being pioneers in the rebirth of Messianic Judaism. The church we were pastoring was basically a Presbyterian church that had Jewish people attending it. The only thing Jewish about it was that we sang the Sh'ma in the beginning and the Aaronic Benediction at the end.[1] We sang from a Presbyterian hymnal that had a Jewish star on it.

The church was originally part of a mission outreach to the Jewish immigrants that came to America in the early 1920s. I believe the church was about forty years old when we took it over in 1972. We arrived there after a church split; the people were wounded and in need of shepherding. Many of the congregants were more than twice our age; it had to be God for them to accept our leadership. They voted us in unanimously! I think there were close to forty who attended regularly at that time. Our one-year internship turned into a six-year stay.

Dan's early sermons were very complicated and hard to understand, but the people loved him anyway. Of course, many of the congregants had problems, so they needed a lot of counseling. It was very hard for us at first. It seemed that this was a place for Jews who really did not want to take up their full identity as Jews, yet they did not feel comfortable in a traditional church. There were even some there who hated being Jewish. We saw our church as a kind of halfway house.

Also, in pioneering a work we found ourselves doing every kind of job imaginable. I had to do the bulletin (I actually drew some pictures on some of them), be the secretary, teach Shabbat school (the Jewish equivalent to Sunday school), head up the nursery, clean up, and plan fellowship meals. God does have a sense of humor, and gradually we learned, though we must have looked awfully funny playing "pastor."

Within a couple years, Dan and some others across the country began to find themselves in agreement over the issue of Jewish assimilation. We came to the conclusion that Jewish people did not have to convert to Christianity—that is, to become Gentile in their practice—in order to believe in Yeshua. Jewish believers themselves could still remain Jewish and practice the Sabbath and feasts and consider themselves part of the restored remnant of Israel. They did not have to eat pork, take on Christian names, sing Christian hymns, attend a denominational church, or stop fellowshipping with their Jewish relatives in order to be saved. This went against the main teaching of the churches of the day—namely replacement theology. Such teaching said God was finished with Israel, and that the church had become the true Israel, a spiritual Israel.

As we began to move forward in our convictions and moved our service from Sunday to Saturday, we received a lot of flak. We even changed the name of our congregation to Adat Ha Tikvah, Congregation of the Hope. Many condemned us as heretics and accused us of rebuilding the wall of partition between Jew and Gentile. Having to stand against such opposition strengthened us and caused us to press even deeper into the heart of God. He was faithful even though we were immature in the beginning stages of the movement.

At first, I think our Jewish pride blew a lot of people away. Then we had internal struggles of discovering who we really were as Jews. We had to answer serious questions like, "What does a believing Jew look like?" or "What should their worship sound like?" Many of us wrestled with these issues through the years, and we were like a pendulum, swinging back and forth to the extremes. At first, we tried to be more like a synagogue. In other words, we tried to do our worship service in such a way that an unbelieving Jew would think and feel like he was in his own synagogue. We would try to do most of our worship in Hebrew and recite many of the same prayers that a Jew would pray from the Jewish prayer book. We tried to be more Jewish in practice than the average Jew.

Next, we swung the other way, becoming like a Gentile church. That is, we did very little Jewish liturgical prayers or had little Jewish content in our worship. An average Christian would experience our services being only a little different from his regular church.

The fleshing out of these identity questions was and is an ongoing endeavor. Even after thirty years of development, many congregations find themselves still trying to solve this challenge. Being a Messianic Jew probably will always mean being caught between two worlds—the world of the church and that of Israel.

We lost a lot of members during the first few months of transitioning our congregation to Messianic Jewish practice. Soon, however, we began to attract the healthier Jews who wanted to be Jews. Music began to develop to express our newfound identity, and a new vocabulary began to emerge: congregation instead of church, Yeshua instead of Jesus, Messiah instead of Christ. Dan and others began to write many books concerning the validity of Messianic Jewish identity, practice, and theology. Many congregations began to spring up all over the country and the world. Slowly, the churches began to accept this new move of God, and many even started to enjoy discovering their own Jewish roots.

However, we always faced a challenge in trying to prevent the pendulum from swinging too far in the church toward the Jewish direction. Some Gentiles felt like second-rate citizens and went overboard in seeking worth trying to act Jewish. Some movements became serious aberrations from the founding fathers of our faith. Increasing pressure was put on the Gentiles to follow Jewish practice—to give up Christmas and Easter, to worship on Saturday instead of Sunday, and to follow biblical kosher laws. But in Christianity there is neither Jew nor Gentile. In the Messiah, we are one; we just have different callings. All the promises given to Abraham were and are for both his natural children as well as for his spiritual children.

During these years, we also returned to the belief and practice of the gifts of the Holy Spirit—out of necessity. We always believed in the indwelling presence of the Holy Spirit from the time of salvation, but we had shied away from the more outward manifestations of the Spirit due to a bad experience we had had during our college days. We did not know if we could trust the source of prophecy, speaking in tongues, or deliverance. How could we discern if something was from God, the devil, or our own imagination? However, in the wisdom of God, we were wooed back to more fully embracing the power of his Spirit in order to enrich his body, the church. Many of our members had been involved in the occult at one time or another. Regular counseling techniques were not able to set them free. We found that praying in tongues increased our spiritual insight to target the oppressor. We found the Bible to be true: we could indeed cast out demons in the name of Yeshua. So our community began to be trained in deliverance ministry, and we grew into a close-knit family.

In the midst of pioneering this new movement, we gave birth to two wonderful children: Ben in March of 1975 and Rebecca in March of 1977. When we had Ben, I had rooming-in at the hospital, which allowed me to care for him from the time he was born. It doesn't seem like much, but this was a new idea at the time. During one of his diaper changes, he stopped breathing.

18 March '75

At 1 p.m. I had my baby for rooming-in. I fed Ben and then later changed his diaper. He had a greenish-black bowel movement. No one told me this was normal, so I was frightened and thought something was wrong with him. I wanted to ask the nurse if he was okay, but then he threw up mucus through his nose and mouth. He tried to breathe, but he couldn't and began choking and turning blue. I got panicky and turned him on his side to try to get him breathing again. I then tilted his head upside down. Still no luck, so I ran out into the hall with him and yelled for help. By the time the nurse arrived, the baby was breathing again. I felt like a fool and was all shaken up. In the afternoon and evening, I was still frightened—how I love Benjamin and just could not bear to lose him. I cried; my nerves were unraveled. Somehow, I had to find courage. Every cry he made worried me; my enjoyment of him changed to fear.

When Dan came, he was so calm. He changed his diaper and sang him to sleep. I was too afraid to even touch him. After Dan left, I forced myself to change another diaper and to feed him some more. At night, I cried again and wondered how I was ever going to be a mother, knowing death is a possibility. I prayed to the LORD and he answered. "Enjoy each minute with Benjamin to the fullest, love him fully, holding back nothing, and then if he does die, be happy for those moments you did love. Quality is what counts and not quantity." If I had loved reservedly out of fear for fifty years, it would not make up for the joy and love (given in abandonment) one can experience for even an hour. How I praise God for being my father and answering my prayers. I now have courage to love no matter how short the time may be. Now I get a small inkling as to how God must have felt after creating man and having seen man hurt himself. You ask whether or not it was worth creating man knowing he would fall, but the joy of those moments when a few respond in love makes it worth it all. There will be moments of worry over colds, falls, behavior problems, and illness while being a mother. Is it worth it? Yes.

This revelation about the importance of fully loving brought comfort to me in 1998 when our youngest child died. Often I had questioned why God had given us Samuel knowing that he would be taken from us twelve years later. However, I was reminded that to love and be loved by another person fully, even for a short time, was worth the pain and suffering of loss.

My fear of losing Ben had its roots in my mother's own loss. Often, she would question out loud whether it was worth having children because of all the pain. It was very difficult for her to embrace life again. I was critical of her back then, but later I understood because I found myself saying the same things.

When I had Becca, I struggled with a different issue. That time I fought the battle of self-centeredness and fears of not being able to love two children.

8 March '77

Well, my hospital "vacation" is almost over. It has been a real time of reflection and fluctuating emotions. I had idealized and looked forward to this time for so long that I have been let down because it did not measure up to my expectations. Whenever you try to recreate the exact joy and excitement of a "first" experience, you will fall flat and end up not experiencing the uniqueness and joy of the new experience. At first, I thought that having a girl would put me on the same high as when I had Ben, but I did have a girl and it still wasn't the same feeling as having a first child. The excitement of birth lasted only a day, and the knowledge of the trials ahead dampened the naïve, romanticized moment. I knew that sleepless nights awaited me and that, once again, I will be tied down for a year, unable to be away from Rebecca for more than a couple of hours. With a first child, this realization is not as vivid.

Another disappointment is that others don't think a second child is that special. You don't have baby showers for your second child. A nice hard and fast rule! Also, no flowers or cards sent to the hospital. Your husband doesn't even seem to treat you special; no flowers or special gifts. I stayed up at night being bitter about this and still find it hard to be reconciled with this lack of interest. I thought about why people aren't showing love toward me. After a while, I began to realize that Dan is showing me love in different ways—by cleaning the house and helping me at home. Life is more than a few cards and flowers. I have such a beautiful daughter who seems to be good-tempered. I also have a unique son who is a once-in-a-lifetime child with such a vibrant and winsome personality, a God-given intelligence, and compassionate nature. Don't these things matter more than flowers or cards? Why is it I have such limited criteria of how I should be loved or blessed when actually I have been showered with blessings?

I also expected this place to be a trysting place like it was the last time—a place to "find God" or renew a relationship with him. I have had no spiritual highs as I did before, but I believe I have learned a lot about myself. Spiritual growth is being able to continue with God through everyday, mundane matters and not question, "Does God love me?" and keep looking for signs. Of course God loves me; I, on the other hand, am the one whose heart turns cold and strays.

Mixing pastoring with parenting small children was very challenging at times for me. Dan was so busy counseling people that he had little time to relieve me of mothering stress. Additionally, I had to get used to not ministering by Dan's side and had to adapt to what appeared to be a less rewarding use of my time. My self-centeredness opened the door to self-pity and bitterness at having to be the one doing most of the parenting. My expectation of parenting was that Dan would change 50 percent of the diapers and even get up in the middle of the night to help soothe a sick child. Then there was the issue of sleeping in. He could sleep as long as he wanted every day, but I had to get up and meet our children's needs. He could leave the house whenever he wanted, but I always had to pack up two babies or find a babysitter when I wanted to go out. I became resentful of his freedom.

25 April '77

I wonder what happened to the "picture postcard" images of motherhood with pink, nude chubby babies pressed against their mother's silky, flowing nightgowns. The mothers are seen sitting in expensively decorated nurseries flooded with sunshine. Oh, the baby clothes that make little babes and motherhood seem so attractive. I wish sometimes that they would dress babies in rags with the smell of spit-up milk on them. And, oh, those perfumed baby products, how can you resist the urge to cuddle a baby of your own with those sweet smells? But, having children is like the rest of life. You have good times and hard times, sometimes more bad than good. Having one child was an adventure. I didn't know what to expect next. I anxiously waited the first smile, word, and step. I was careful to note the date and time of each new achievement for posterity. I felt such a special bond with my little boy almost immediately, even though he was difficult at times. It was bearable, though, because all my affections were tied up in him.

Perhaps my greater difficulty with him was that I tried to follow Le Leche League's advice of nursing on demand and never letting your child cry. I felt so guilty when I would let him cry because it was impossible to hold him all the time. I went through so many guilt trips trying to be the perfect mother. I am ingrained with the fears that with one slip-up I could make a criminal out of my child.

Then there were the illnesses. Benji would get so sick—105-degree temperatures. Oh, how I would have to rely on God!

Perhaps my greatest adjustment was getting used to being tied down and not being able to sleep when I wanted. I love sleep—I even prayed God would cure me of it.

With my second, I am more relaxed but I still worry about sleep. I am not so guilty over letting her cry as I was with Benji. Perhaps it is because it is impossible to always hold her when there is another child. I am having a hard time keeping the same level of love as with my first child. I feel so bad when I am antagonistic toward Benji when he misbehaves; it is as if our unique relationship is being destroyed. I miss the closeness we once had. Now I cannot be really close with either one. I find myself so busy that I am not even playing with Rebecca like I should. I am so anxious to put her down so I can be with Benji and try to hold onto what we once had. I hope it doesn't disappear completely. I wonder if it is really possible to love two children, each in a special way. I wonder how large families ever manage. I know I didn't feel neglected even though I am the third child of my parents in two years. Perhaps children don't need as much individual attention as I think they do but need quality time instead, even if it is for an hour. I have to be creative and plan special times.

I think mothering would be much more pleasant if I would accept my limited freedom and count it a joy to be able to raise two beautiful human beings. I complain too much, and yet my trials are so small. I have to be tougher, more patient, and per-severing or I will crumble when things really get rough. I need to grow closer to God more than ever. If I were to become a better person, more like the Messiah, then mothering will take care of itself. I want to provide a good atmosphere for my husband and family, but sometimes it seems impossible.

Prayer

God, help me to be an instrument of peace instead of creating more tension. Help me to develop the right attitude and instill in me patience and courage for hard times. Help me not to love sleep or "freedom" above your will for me. Forgive me for my bitter feelings toward your children—your gifts—and for mistreating them sometimes. LORD, let their lives be dependent on you, and may my mistakes not ruin the attitudes they might have toward you. Help me to raise them to love you, and if you should take them before I deem right, help me not to be bitter or make harsh, quick decisions I'd later be sorry for. It is hard being a mother. I don't want it unless you are with me ... too much is at stake. Help me to love the present and not always be anxious for the future, or I'll be sad about the past. I need your love—do not forsake me or let me forsake you. I love you ... mold me and make me. Amen.

I am happy to say that I did learn to love two children, and my love was not divided in two, but rather my capacity to love was multiplied. Also, my children did not grow up to be criminals despite our many mistakes (and we did a lot of repenting). We learned to keep the communication lines open in our home.

Flashed Forward

By day the LORD went ahead of them in a pillar of cloud to guide
them on their way and by night in a pillar of fire to give them
light, so that they could travel by day or night.

Exodus 13:21

I loved our home in Chicago. We had almost forty people from our congregation living within walking distance of one another. My best friend lived down the block, and we were looking forward to raising our children together. We loved community. God was fulfilling this part of our life vision, even the part of living in the midst of a conservative to orthodox Jewish community.

Everything was within walking distance—the neighborhood bakery, butcher, and deli. We fit right in. We were up to over eighty people in attendance, and we genuinely were happy. Then came the call to come to Washington, D.C. to candidate for a position that was open at Beth Messiah.

"No, not now, LORD! We have worked too hard to get to the place where we are comfortable." We thought we would just go there and speak on some Friday and Sunday and enjoy the free visit to D.C. After all, we would have to hear from God if we were to uproot ourselves.

During the spring of 1977, we flew down to D.C. and spent a few days with the people of Beth Messiah. They wined and dined us by having us spend time in different elders' homes. I was shocked to find out how far apart each member lived. We drove an hour in this direction and then an hour and a half in the other direction. They were spread out all over the beltway. I told Dan one night how thankful I was that God wasn't calling us there. Our vision was community, and I told God I would never live in the suburbs. But then it happened.

On Sunday afternoon they had a baptism in a pool at an elder's home. We had a picnic and sat around and worshiped and talked. As I looked at the people, I saw them as sheep without a shepherd. My heart, as well as Dan's, softened. My shepherd's heart transferred from Chicago to Washington at that very moment. After praying for a few months and taking time to get confirmation, the impossible happened—we moved to the suburbs of Washington, D.C. that next January. Ben was three, and Becca was one. On our moving day, Becca was running a fever and threw up all over her snowsuit. We had to travel all the distance with her vomiting, having diarrhea, and crying. On top of all this, there was a bad snowstorm. We wondered whether we had really heard God. By the time we arrived, Becca had a 105-degree fever, but one of the congregants activated their prayer chain and she was soon healed.

When it came time to move into our new home, we found that the basement had six inches of water in it. The owner said it had never happened before. We found that doing the will of God wasn't always easy and, sometimes, the sign of being in his will is the opposition we face in trying to walk out our obedience.

The early days at Beth Messiah nearly burned us out. Dan made the mistake of preaching a version of "Come unto me all you who are weary and heavy laden." And come they did. We received as many as thirty-five calls a day and over five hundred calls in one month. Counseling seemed to be our main occupation since the church's painful split a year before we arrived. There were still many factions and much disunity left over. We found ourselves in a precarious situation once again where we had to deal with many hurting people.

Because Dan let the needs of the members dictate his hours, he began to neglect the family. We eventually learned we were not God to them and began to pace ourselves. We learned from other pastors how to give ourselves to training leaders instead of counseling each member one at a time; we had to equip the leaders to minister rather than doing all the work ourselves. This was very important to future ministry.

God began to send us gifted young men who were zealous for him, beginning in 1979. They became Dan's right and left arms. God also sent us talented musicians who later became a famous singing group, Israel's Hope. Beth Messiah was put on the map

and became one of the "in" Messianic Jewish congregations during the early '80s. We even started a Messianic Jewish Day School,
Ets Chaiyim, of which I was the first principal.

Life became very full, and sometimes our walk with the LORD
suffered. The quiet times seemed to shorten. Some days, we even
missed devotions as the mornings filled up with appointments.
We had grown too fast and began to make decisions without
enough prayer and clear direction. If it weren't for the grace of
God working through the faithfulness of our associate pastors
and other steadfast elders, I think we would have shipwrecked
our congregation. Many people were sent out before replace-
ments were raised up to fill their area of service. Misinterpreting
the timing of implementing new directions—and quite a bit of
pride—got us into trouble.

In retrospect, it seems God might have been in the mistakes to
humble us. He often brings us through desert experiences to reveal
what is in our heart. Today, we have learned to wait on him for
direction and timing before moving on, which is basically the fear
of the LORD. We are grateful for both good times and bad and for
the many friendships that have enriched each step of the way.

Shining Hope

When I said, "My foot is slipping," your love, O Lord, supported me. When anxiety was great within me, your consolation brought joy to my soul.

Psalm 94:18–19

My comfort in my suffering is this: your promise preserves my life.

Psalm 119:50

By this time I was having consistent prophetic dreams, but I was not paying too much attention to them. One night God interrupted my regular flow of dreaming with an announcement. He said I would have a son and that he should be called *Shmuel Capha*, Samuel Peter. I was told that none of his words would fall to the ground and that I was to watch over this word. I saw my son in front of large crowds doing mighty signs and wonders. I believed that God had created him to be a prophetic evangelist. I had to keep this dream in my heart, knowing that only God could change my husband's heart toward having more children.

Dan still had the sixties mind-set of zero population growth. He believed couples should have no more than two children so as not to overpopulate the world. For this reason, when I had a dream in the fall of 1981 about having another child, he did not believe it and said God was going to have to tell him.

In the spring of 1982, while I was still the principal of Ets Chaiyim, I reached a place of burnout. Working full time and coming home to be a mother, wife, and minister took its toll. My spiritual life almost dried up. I was desperate for some downtime but did not see how that would be possible.

One morning I told one of our part-time teachers to take over for me because I had to pray. I went up to the front of the sanctuary of our congregational building and lay facedown on the carpet. In great distress, I began to cry and pour out my heart to God. How I missed my times with him, and I hungered for more fellowship. I felt so dry and trapped and saw no way out of my intense schedule. God heard my prayers and answered them in a way I did not expect.

Within two weeks, I developed a bad case of bronchitis along with a severe cough. During one of the coughing spells, I felt a stabbing pain in my back, almost like a knife was thrust in me. I tried to ignore the pain and carry on. For a whole week I continued my busy schedule, pushing myself despite the increased muscle spasms and pain going down my back and left leg. On the weekend, I even sat through over twenty hours of meetings. By Monday morning, when I got out of bed, I could not feel the bottom of my left foot. I immediately made an appointment with an orthopedic doctor. After a few tests, he looked at me and said he was putting me into the hospital right then and there. I broke into tears.

I was plagued by my concerns over the school and my children. (Ben was seven at the time, and Becca was five.) I wondered who would take care of all my responsibilities. And then I thought about Dan and the burden my absence would lay upon him. He already had too much to do. Who would have dreamed that one cough could suddenly free me from my impossible schedule!

Soon, I was wheeled into the hospital and put into traction. The doctors were upset with me for waiting so long to get help. Each day brought no improvement. Many friends came to visit and tried to comfort me. God was already at work and taught me that his grace was sufficient for any trial I might find myself in. I was not afraid; his peace filled the room. Many prayed for me all across the country, and it felt like I was being carried along in his arms.

After I had been in the hospital for two weeks, God spoke to me.

27 *March '82*

"This shaking process is from me; do not rebuke Satan. Pray for endurance and the whole armor of God that you will be able to withstand the darts of Satan tempting you to get bitter and angry with me or to indulge in self-pity. I am purging you. Praise my name, for I care for you; I love you with an everlasting love. I would not give you these trials and tribulations if I were not already prepared to deliver you, whether it be financial difficulties, physical ailments, or personal loss. I have said that, in the last days, few will persevere and endure to the end. I pray that all of you will be able to remain steadfast. The end times are coming fast. There isn't much time to get you ready—hence the trials. Please trust me; you will come through victorious! Satan will only get a foothold if you take your eyes away from me and stop trusting me. I know what I am doing—I created you, didn't I? I created the world, the stars, and all that exists. Because I love you, you will endure, and through enduring you will grow into maturity, producing every kind of fruit that is beneficial to those around you. There is no other way. Let me mold you and make you, even if it hurts. My ways are bigger than your ways. Oh, just trust my love for you. I will carry you when the load gets too heavy."

I will shout praises to God. He will deliver! He will provide; He will give strength! The LORD will fulfill his purpose for me.

Oh God, your love endures forever. Do not abandon the works of your hands. Your goal is faith. Suffering has come so that faith may prove genuine and may result in praise, glory, and honor upon Yeshua's return. Yeshua entrusted himself to you while he was suffering unjustly because he knew that you judge justly. After I have suffered a little while, you will restore me, making me strong and steadfast. Your divine power has given me everything I need for life and godliness.

On March 31, I had a myelogram, a test in which dye was injected into my spinal column, and then X-rays were made to determine if there was a blockage. Typically, it can be quite frightening since the doctor has to stick a needle between two vertebrae and position it exactly in the spinal fluid. One slip and he could hit the main spinal nerves. God gave me such peace that, again, there was no fear. They discovered that a piece of disk had broken off and was protruding into my spinal column, causing paralysis. An emergency operation was scheduled for the very next day—my birthday.

God ministered to me throughout the night and into the morning. When the nurse came in to administer a sedative, she found me crying and asked if I was all right. She did not know that I was crying because of the goodness of the LORD and his sweet presence that was enfolding me. Recovery from surgery was very painful and stretched out over several months. By the time I went to the doctor for help, I had already greatly bruised my nerves, so healing was long and slow. It was a strange handicap since I could not sit for long, stand for long, or even lie down in any one position for very long. I was in constant back pain and had to take several different kinds of painkillers. Many times, I would try to eat dinner with my family, only to have to retire to bed after a few minutes. The pain was constant and made me very self-focused, as it took strength not to give into the pain and fall apart. For six months, I spent most of my time in bed. Different people served as live-in helpers, and many others provided meals. When I went to church services, I had to lie down on a couch in the back of the sanctuary.

God had set me apart and caused me to lie down in green pastures. There he restored my soul and imparted to me a compassion for the sick and hurting. He accomplished a lot in my family during that year. I wrote much during this time because I believed it was a turning point for me.

6 April '82

Trials remind me of when I used to go fishing with my father. We were always getting our lines tangled, and made it worse by our frantic efforts to undo the tangle. It took Dad's patient hands to free the lines, since we had to wait patiently on the bank of the stream. We could not wait to get back to fishing. In the same way, in our anxiety to go about our "calling," we often get caught up in trials that hinder us from going forward in our calling. Trials are as much a part of our calling as our ministry and regular tasks, just as tangled lines and fishing are part of the same adventure. We must wait patiently on the riverbank until our heavenly father untangles our fishing lines so we can get back to fishing.

7 *April '82*

As I was praying this morning, there was a special anointing. God was speaking tenderly to me. I was seeking my new role, and he told me I was to be a nurse to people's souls. Their souls would be laid bare before me, and God would give me insight, wisdom, and direction for bringing healing. I bawled. I had wanted to be a nurse as a child and sometimes had felt like I missed my calling (also my calling as a missionary). God has tied both of these two desires together. Praise his name! May I be worthy of this high calling. Oh LORD, guide and direct me. Fulfill these words and speak loudly to me so I may hear you. I want only you; I want to be your servant and your friend. Discern my motives and purify those that are selfish. Praise your name.

Even now, at the time of this writing, I am overcome with gratefulness. God has been so good to me; his mercies truly are new every morning. His faithfulness knows no boundaries. How healing it is to recount the stories of his goodness in my life throughout the years.

7 *April '82*

Tonight I was gripped with the fear of dying, but God greatly comforted me. I had taken too many aspirins for pain; my stomach was upset, my pulse was fast and erratic, and my breathing labored. I feared not being able to breathe, even feared going to sleep. I knew it was an attack from Satan because I had experienced this attack before; Dan had to hold me and pray for me. This time Dan was not around, and I had to face these fears alone. I cried out to God, and he heard my voice. He directed me to turn to Psalm 18. What a great chapter for those under attack! It talked about cords of death surrounding someone and them crying out to God. God was angry that the enemy was tormenting the one he took delight in. He thundered from his mighty hill and came down and shot the enemy with his arrows. He became my shield, my victory, my rock, and refuge. I cried from relief to know that God gets angry with Satan when he attacks us, and that he will come and defend us. It took a while, but he shot every one of my fears. I have faced death, and God won! Praise his name! I slept peacefully finally. But what a spiritual battle.

The doctors became concerned because I was not healing the way they thought I should. They could not figure out why I was in so much pain, so they decided to put me in the hospital for more tests at the end of April. Even though this trial tested me daily, God continually showed himself faithful. It is hard to explain to someone how I could be in so much pain yet receive so much grace to endure. I learned that I could go through anything, as long as God's presence sustained me. Through that entire year, when I was in so much pain, I can't remember his allowing me to stay depressed for too long without encouraging me.

The next journal entry reveals my ongoing battle to maintain a sense of God's presence and the doubts I would go through when I did not feel him. The first visit to the hospital in March had lasted two weeks, but this second visit lasted only one week. Learning to walk by faith is a battle, indeed. God, again in his mercy, revealed himself in a dream and encouraged me to continue running after him.

9 June '82

Oh, LORD, my LORD, how majestic are your ways. They are far above my understanding. Why did you allow such intimacy during the first seven weeks of my back problem but now it is not as before? Do I need to be in constant trial to be that close? My soul is restless and is not satisfied with macaroni and cheese after eating steak. Am I only seeking after "feeling" and not you? The time we had together was like that of a romantic movie. How intense our relationship was. I long for it. I had immediate access to your throne. Now, I have to struggle to maintain prayer, worship, and communion with you. Show me what can be expected in my daily walk with you. Are my expectations too high? Has sin separated me from you? Have I bragged about my treasures as did Hezekiah and now have lost them? I know you haven't abandoned me, but there is a barrier. Do I have an idol in my life? Oh, God, I desire such closeness that I can walk and talk with you as Adam and Eve did. I desire your wisdom to know how to speak into the needs of others. I want to have words of praise upon my lips continuously. Is it possible to be always aware of your presence? Is being aware of your presence only a "feeling" and not to be sought after? Of course, your presence is always around us but is it wrong to want to feel you all the time? LORD, give me confidence in your promises that the work you have started in me will be brought to completion, that you will never leave me nor forsake me. I am happiest when I sense you are using me to further your kingdom. It doesn't have to be big and noticeable, just you answering my prayers gives me such joy. I love it when you give me a burden to pray for someone and your spirit groans within me for them. The experience of travailing in prayer until it lifts, and then knowing that you have answered, gives me joy.

During this period, many people began to give me books on faith to read that encouraged me to believe for a complete healing of my back. I spent a lot of time reading Kenneth Hagin, T.L. Osborne, Smith Wigglesworth, and John G. Lake—anything I could get my hands on. Soon I began to eat, drink, and sleep thinking about laying hands on the sick and seeing them recover. There were so many questions I had to wrestle through, though.

One man of God who came to speak at Beth Messiah challenged me by asking, "Do you believe that God caused this injury to your back?" I looked at him with shock.

"Of course God caused this injury," I said, "because look at all the good that has come from it." He, in turn, was shocked with my answer, as he firmly believed that a good God does not put sickness on his children. (Yet many times in the Word I have found where God does put sickness on his children for chastisement or discipline.) He said it was always God's will to heal, just like it was always God's will that none should perish. This shook up my theology because I believed in the sovereignty of God—all that happens to mankind is ultimately under his control.

I couldn't come to peace with a theology on healing back then, and I am still wrestling with these issues today. God's Word is true, and his promises concerning healing are true, but faith is a mystery. The Bible says that faith comes by hearing and hearing comes by the word of God, but who opens our ears so that we can hear the word of faith? In Isaiah 6:9–10, God speaks a curse over the Israelites: "Be ever hearing, but never understanding; be ever seeing, but never perceiving. Make the heart of this people calloused; make their ears dull and close their eyes. Otherwise they might see with their eyes, hear with their ears, understand with their hearts, and turn and be healed." Yet we are told in the Word, "Be it unto you according to your faith." How much of healing faith is a gift of God, and how much of healing faith can we obtain through our own effort? Yeshua only did what he saw his father doing and only spoke what he heard his father speaking. Therefore, he had perfect results. It seems God is in charge of opening and closing our spiritual ears and eyes.

I do know one thing, however; God's grace, manifesting itself in patient endurance, sustained me through that year's long trial. I even had to go into the hospital for another myelogram. This time, because of the bruised nerves, the procedure was extremely painful. The recovery that night was almost unbearable since I could not lie completely flat due to the dye injected into my spinal column and because I was forced to lie in the most painful position for my back injury. I ended up pacing my room and crying until the nurse finally gave me some morphine.

No doctor gave me hope of ever being free from pain. The months of waiting for healing stretched out until April of 1983— almost a full year. We were encouraged by Sid Roth to go to a Winter Bible Seminar at Rhema Bible Institute to hear Kenneth Hagin speak on intercession. Though we knew the trip on the plane would be painful for me, we decided to go.

Each morning they conducted a healing school for those who were sick. That very first morning, during the worship time, the woman leading worship stopped and said, "I sense someone here has just been healed. Get up and do what you couldn't do before." Before that time, all I could do was bend over to touch my knees, and even though I didn't feel any strange anointing, I somehow knew she was speaking to me. I jumped to my feet and bent over to touch my toes. My joy knew no limits—God had healed my back!

The worship leader had me come forward to testify. From that time on, I was healed of chronic pain and was able to sit through over twenty hours of meetings that week. I never would have dreamed that healing could come so quickly or unexpectedly. There was no struggle for faith; it just happened because I was in an atmosphere of faith where there was an open heaven for healing to take place—many people through the years had been healed in that very room where I was healed.

Another miracle happened while we were at Rhema—I got pregnant. Surely, I thought, this was the fulfillment of the dream I had back in the fall of 1981. I was confident that this baby was Samuel, so Dan and I continued to talk to "Samuel" in my womb as we excitedly awaited his arrival.

Looking back on that year of forced sabbatical, I can see how it was a time of preparation for the days ahead. So much of God's Word took root in me, and his compassion for the sick became strong in me. God released me into a six-year season of receiving powerful, prophetic word-of-knowledge dreams that found their fulfillment at services Saturday morning where I would call the people forward whom I had seen in my dream. I would then pray for them, and often they would be healed.

Also, during that time, I began to experience powerful manifestations of the Holy Spirit. Often, I would fall when praying for people because the Spirit's power was greater than I could handle. This was before manifestations of the Holy Spirit (such as shaking, groaning, travailing, laughing, falling down, and others) were made commonplace through the Toronto and Pensacola outpourings of the Spirit. (These kinds of manifestations were also present during various revivals throughout church history.) Dan did not know what to do with me and would often say, "Patty, you really have to learn to control yourself." I would look at him and think, *Yeah, right. I'd like to see you stand up under God's power.* Thankfully, I had an eldership overseeing me that hungered for God as much as I did and wanted to see him show up in power. They were very patient with me. We learned together how to govern these outpourings so people would be edified and blessed.

Admittedly, my zeal would often lack wisdom and did freak people out and perhaps scare them away from pursuing the workings of the Holy Spirit in their lives. But many were blessed by the work of the Spirit during this time.

Luminary Visions

I will go on to visions and revelations from the LORD. I know a man in Christ who fourteen years ago was caught up to the third heaven. Whether it was in the body or out of the body I do not know—God knows.

2 Corinthians 12:1–2

Dan and I were excited as the birth of Samuel drew near. People were joking with us about what we would do if the baby turned out to be a girl. Would we call her Samantha? This did not seem remotely possible to me because my dreams were rarely wrong. One of my close friends had a strong sense that the baby was going to be a girl, so she prayed that when I saw her I would be filled with joy.

I finally gave birth on January 18, 1984. The delivery was easy. As the baby was being pushed out, Dan exclaimed, "Oh Patty, it's a boy—oops, I mean a girl." I was shocked. But then they placed this precious baby in my arms. She did not cry, but pushed her little fists down into me and looked me straight in the eye. I exploded with tears of joy. She was so beautiful, and it did not matter that she wasn't a boy. We immediately bonded in such a deep and lasting way.

The next morning, when they brought her to me, I again burst into tears because she filled my heart with such joy. I had a vision of her dancing in Israel—so full of life and happiness. We all wondered what we would name this little surprise. How strange it was not to have a name for her for five days. Soon, it became obvious that there was only one name for her: Simcha Naomi, which is Hebrew for "my pleasant joy." She has more than ful-filled the meaning of her name, as she has been a joy and delight in bringing life back into our souls after Sam's death. But I still pondered in my heart the meaning of the dream about Samuel—was there still another baby yet to come?

During this period, I recorded what came to be the birth and growth of a season of supernatural workings in my life.

5 April '85

It has been a lifelong pursuit to experience God the way the people of the Bible experienced him. So many times I have hungered to such great depths only to be frustrated. What I was hungering after was not forthcoming. Then I would go through a time of dryness and discouragement. Why wasn't the lifestyle of biblical times possible for today, for me? I wanted all of it. I wanted to experience the depths of God, almost being consumed by the relationship so that people would only see him, not me. I wanted the verse about doing greater miracles to be a reality in my life. I wanted the lame to walk, the blind to see, and the depressed to be set free. Why weren't they? How do you get such faith to lay hands on people? I wanted that kind of walk with God. I began to dream about laying hands on people, praying in tongues for them, and then the sick becoming healed and delivered. How I longed for my dreams to become a reality.

About three and one half years ago (the time of my back injury) I began to seriously seek the LORD. I read books on miracles, and I wept because I wasn't experiencing the same life. Then I became angry when I was on my back in pain from the surgery. I had a lot of time to reflect and felt close to God, but this bit about healing was evading me, so I threw the books aside. However, through my own ongoing suffering, God increased my compassion for others who were suffering. I became desperate in my powerlessness to relieve my own distress as well as others' afflictions. Life had to be better than what I was experiencing. The Bible certainly painted a different picture for those who were sick than with what I was familiar. Yeshua and his disciples healed the sick, cast out demons, and raised the dead. Why couldn't I? I had to press through.

I read *Christ the Healer* by Bosworth, and this convinced me that healing was for everyone. More books and tapes followed. I began to see that what I hungered after was possible. I gobbled up everything I could get my hands on that dealt with healing. Gradually, some of this teaching went deep into my heart.

During the last five or six years, I have had several prophetic dreams, especially about the formation of Ets Chaiyim School. Also, I began to move in words of knowledge. I remember going to a women's conference in 1983, and I started feeling the LORD speak to me about a woman who was present there who had attempted or was about to attempt suicide. He proceeded to tell me that her name began with the letter "C," she had blonde hair, and she was a pastor's wife. To my utter amazement, a woman who perfectly fit the description came forward in tears when I was released to give the word publicly. However, I was not moving in the supernatural on a consistent basis. It was too sporadic to satisfy—what was holding me back?

On March 29, 1985, a special speaker came to our congregation to minister. On Friday night, he stayed with us. I picked his brain, trying to discover how to move in the realm of the supernatural. He told me that I was moving in the prophetic realm and the fear of man was holding me back. I had prayer for deliverance from guilt and fear, and I knew something happened.

The next day at service, another gentleman had a word of knowledge for me. He said that I should be moving in the prophetic ministry, but the fear of man was holding me back. He spoke almost word for word what the speaker had spoken the night before.

After the message, the speaker began to pray for people who had needs, encouraging them to expect God to work in mighty ways. Nothing unusual was happening, and again I felt frustrated. I wanted the power of God to fall in a mighty way, but it wasn't. I started to pray for the minister to move in a greater anointing. All of a sudden, I began to feel fiery warmth grow in intensity in my hands and body. I figured that this feeling must be what the faith teachers referred to as the anointing. I knew I had to go up front and pray for the people. I stood behind one of my students from school and later moved to be in front of her. When I put my hand on her head, the power of God exploded in me, and I began to pray in tongues wildly. Suddenly, I felt a surge of power go through me, and we both fell to the ground (or were thrown to the ground would be more accurate). I've never experienced anything like this before, only in my dreams. I wanted to stay on the ground, but God told me to pray for others. I got up and began to pray for another woman, but I started shaking and praying in tongues. I prayed for a few moments wildly and was attacked by a fear thought—she probably thinks I am crazy. (What happened to being delivered from the fear of man?) I had to fight that thought, and the anointing left. I was discouraged because the anointing lifted, yet I knew I had broken through. I was beginning a new level of walking with God. I felt like Mary, who pondered in her heart the words spoken to her. God became even more precious to me.

I knew I had to now set my face like flint and continue to press into God in prayer and study his Word. It is as if I saw a monster and ran into my parents' arms for protection. Now, I must not leave his side because his power is dangerous if used wrongly, out of a wrong motive. I needed to be even more purified and responsible in my walk with God.

It is very difficult to explain the deep joy I feel. I feel like I have come to the end of a long journey of running after God and now am beginning a new and more exciting journey. What was a dream of hope has become a reality. God does indeed live within us—through his spirit. Now is the time to grow deeper into the knowledge of him, to reflect upon and ponder at the wonder of it all. I don't ever want to come off this mountain into dryness again. LORD, give me the grace to seek you daily. I want your praises to always be upon my lips and for there to be no barriers of sin between us.

Prayer

Oh, how I love you, God. Your mercies endure forever. You are the same yesterday and today. You satisfy the hunger of those who seek you. Help me to not be puffed up with pride but to use this gift wisely. I don't want to flaunt it. Help me to be a stronger receptor of your power and not lose sight of your compassion for the people—the reason for your redemptive power. Oh, how I love to be used by you to minister life to people. There is no greater joy!

These manifestations may seem ordinary now, but they were not common in 1985 and I suffered greatly from the reproach of men. Often, I would get attacked with thoughts of shame because of the "strangeness" of these manifestations. Sometimes I would feel like I failed God in not giving the word exactly the way he might have wanted it given.

To give you a better idea of the goodness of God during this season of my life, I am going to write a few of the dreams with their fulfillment. Some have said that the reason God spoke to me in dreams so much was because I never sat still long enough for him to speak to me while I was awake. If you knew me, you might agree. May you be blessed with the realization that God cares so much for us that he will even give a mother and housewife dreams so she can be used to deliver a gift of grace to people in need.

Fall of '85

I dreamed of a woman with great emotional distress who was having difficulty becoming stable spiritually. I prayed in tongues over her, and God revealed to me that it had to do with something her mother had failed to do. When I awoke, I asked God the meaning of this, and I thought he said that her mother did not visit her in the hospital, but I dismissed it because it was too close to what had happened to my sister when she was young.

The Fulfillment

The next Saturday, I came under the unction of the spirit and made known my dream without the details about the hospital. I was afraid of being wrong because it was so specific. A woman immediately came forward in tears, sobbing heavily. She said that when she was little she was in an auto accident, and as a result she ended up in the hospital for three months. Her mother never visited her, and when she returned home, her mother was drunk. The woman received prayer and forgave her mother.

13 August '86

I dreamed of a young mother who had stomach cancer and was dying. She had two small children who were grieving; a son who was especially close was hurting deeply. Then I dreamed that I was before the conference and made known the dream and a middle-aged woman responded. I was puzzled at the discrepancy of the two different ages of the women in my dream. I prayed for her in my dream, and she was healed.

The Fulfillment

Two days later at our annual conference, I could not worship and felt that I should tell the dream. A middle-aged woman responded who said she had stomach cancer; she also said she had children and grandchildren. I prayed for her. Later, I found out that she attended one of the congregations near us. When Dan and I went there to speak, she reminded us who she was and said she had been healed. She had had an operation earlier, and a cancerous tumor was removed. Another operation was scheduled (after the conference) to remove part of her stomach and the surrounding tissue. Shortly after the conference, she went into surgery, but when they opened her up they found no trace of abnormal tissue. She was totally healed! She knew it was God.

29 October '86

I had a dream about a man in our congregation. He was surrounded by volumes of journals he had written about his life, and he asked me to read them. As I started reading the first book, I saw a little baby out in the field crying to be picked up, almost feeling like an aborted or abandoned baby. He wanted to be hugged and affirmed. The rest of the books were filled with more of his hurts of not finding acceptance and approval, especially from his father. I saw a lot of beatings and other abuses—a lonely child who wanted so desperately to be loved. At the end of the dream, God said he wanted the man to throw away these volumes and look to him for approval. God was pleased with him and desired to release him into a new sense of manhood. A new area of ministry would open up. His looking to his earthly father for approval and holding onto his past has held him back from growing up.

The Fulfillment

On Saturday, I called the man forward whom I had seen in my dream and gave him the details of it. He received the word as being accurate and said it fit him 100 percent. He had indeed written many journals about his hurts and said God had told him to throw the journals out the night before, but he had not done it yet. I prayed for him, and he received a powerful touch from the LORD. The following week he brought these hardbound journals to services and testified of his newfound freedom. This man later became an emissary (missionary) in the former Soviet Union and fathered several congregations.

30 October '86

I dreamed I was in the Beth Messiah congregation and God gave me a word of knowledge about how he wanted to heal people's ears this morning. I sensed he wanted to restore hearing to fluid-filled and nerve-damaged ears, especially in right ears. He told me to be more controlled and to hold myself back as I ministered, to be very detailed in instructing people. I awoke but knew the dream was from God because of the sense of anointing in the dream.

The Fulfillment

On Saturday, November 1, I went forward to deliver the word at the appropriate time. I began by encouraging the people about the woman who had stomach cancer and was healed supernaturally. Then, I exhorted them more about believing for God to act and gave my dream as the LORD had instructed.

God's anointing was so strong that I was confident he would carry out his word.

Many people came forward. I prayed first for a small boy who had definite hearing loss and was diagnosed with having a hearing deformity. The parents later gave testimony of their son being healed.

These were thrilling times for me and for the congregation. But then, in 1989, the frequency of prophetic dreams began to diminish, and I rarely moved in powerful anointing for healing. Most of the prophetic words then were about sensing what the spirit wanted to do for a particular time or season in our congregation or where Dan and I happened to be speaking. These words have been accurate, yet how I have longed to return to the ministry of setting the captives free in the name of Yeshua. There was a period of about a year when a team of five (including myself) from our congregation worked intensely on deliverance and inner healing, but the fruit was minimal. The people receiving ministry often did not combine their healing with a continued daily embracing of the cross in their lives. I slowly began to lose my confidence. I wondered what went wrong.

Then, at the end of 1988 and on into 1989, there was a man who attended our congregation who was suffering from an inoperable brain tumor. Before he attended our congregation for the first time, I had had a dream about a man with a head tumor. In the dream, I saw him living in fear of this "thing" that had entered his head. I had seen a dark, demon-like creature enter into the side of the head where the tumor was located. In my dream I confronted the man and roared with the roar of the lion of Judah and told him that God was the one whom he was to fear. The fear of the LORD drove out this dark "creature," and he was healed.

On the following Saturday, I gave the word and found the fulfillment of the word in this man. Then, there began a long struggle for his life. Many times over the next two years, I had supernatural, confirming words and dreams concerning this man and his healing. The doctors gave him no hope to live beyond a couple of months, yet he lived for almost two years from the time he came to Beth Messiah. Periodically, he would go into a coma, and we thought that it was the end. We brought together many prayer warriors, praying he would be raised from his sick bed. In December of 1989, he entered into a coma from which he never recovered; several of us were in his room when he took his last breath. For the next several hours, we tried to raise him from the dead. After all, how could all those supernatural words be wrong? How foolish we must have looked, but we were zealous in our faith. His death was a blow to our congregation. It felt like running into a brick wall at full speed. We were all shocked that he was not healed.

Shortly after this incident, we were caught up in another life and death battle, this time for a little girl's life. She had a spinal tumor that was inoperable, so again it was a matter of "waiting" for her to die but still fighting for her life through prayer and fasting. This time, I did not enter into the battle wholeheartedly because I was still reeling from the past "failure." I was reluctant to experience that kind of painful disappointment. I reasoned, "Why spend myself on something that I am no longer confident will work? If it is not God's will to heal all the time, how do I know what battle to enter into?" The breath was knocked out of us, and it was a struggle for us to regain our zeal for healing faith again. Of course, there were other deaths we would witness later; these too took their toll on our faith for healing.

Looming Threat

"Do I bring to the moment of birth and not give delivery?" says the LORD. "Do I close up the womb when I bring to delivery?" says your God. "Rejoice with Jerusalem and be glad for her, all you who love her; rejoice greatly with her, all you who mourn over her. For you will nurse and be satisfied at her comforting breasts; you will drink deeply and delight in her overflowing abundance."

Isaiah 66:9–11

Dan finally relented and threw away his sixties population growth mentality. After all, he reasoned, his good friend decided not to have children, so we were just using up their allotment of two children. So, in January of 1985, I got pregnant. Surely this one had to be Samuel, but eight weeks into the pregnancy, I miscarried. I was devastated. Where was our promised Samuel?

For those who have never had a miscarriage, it is hard to understand how a woman can go through all the stages of grieving when she never even had relationship with the baby outside the womb. But I did grieve; and I went through all the stages of anger, unbelief, depression, and sadness, except it lasted only a few days. There was life inside of me, and then it was gone. As soon as I found out I was pregnant, I began bonding with that child. My thoughts began to think of the future, of the day I would hold that precious life in my arms. "Samuel" was already a part of my life. When I miscarried, my hope and love both grieved.

Six months went by, and Dan and I were not able to get pregnant again. I didn't understand why, since I had never had a problem conceiving before. In June of 1985, I told God that I did not want to base my life on the dream of Samuel and said that if I did not get pregnant that month, I wanted to close up shop. I did not want any children after I turned thirty-six. (Don't you like the way we talk to God sometimes and give him ultimatums? We're pretty nervy!) That month, I became pregnant. God apparently tolerated my insolence and immaturity. He was so patient with me.

The pregnancy was pretty uneventful. With this birth, Dan and I had felt led of the LORD to have a home birth. We were blessed to have two believing midwives to assist in the delivery.

On Friday, March 28, I started going into labor. I called the midwives and some of my close friends to be present as intercessors. When the midwife first checked me, I immediately dilated to seven centimeters. We played worship music in the background and audiotaped the event. The labor was slow but not difficult. It wasn't until about two the next morning that I began to go through transition. I even took a shower in the midst of transition to speed things up! I could not figure out why it was taking so long, as my other labors were relatively short.

We called our two older children in at this point to share in the joy. Ben was eleven at this time, and Becca was nine. When it came time to push, the midwife turned to the intercessors and said, "Begin to pray. We have a problem. One of the baby's hands is coming out with the head. I have to make a decision whether to push the hand back in or pull it out first." I had to stop pushing until the midwife finally decided to pull the hand out. Then the baby was delivered quite easily into the hands of Dan. We all burst into tears and shouts of joy when we discovered a beautiful baby boy! Samuel Peter Juster was here at last—the dream came true and only three days before my thirty-sixth birthday!

Suddenly, the midwife began to move quickly because she found a true knot in the umbilical cord. Ben had to cut the cord right away. She said that the hand on Sam's head during delivery slowed down the labor process and probably saved his life. It seemed that even at Samuel's birth Satan tried to take his life.

Samuel was born on Shabbat (Saturday) morning, which, according to Jewish tradition, is considered a blessing. I had always wanted to be a recipient of this blessing so that we could do the circumcision on the following Shabbat (on the eighth day). The following Saturday, Sam's circumcision was performed at our regular weekly celebration (but not in front of everyone!). He received many prophetic prayers from the elders at that time. The ceremony proved very special and meaningful to all of those in attendance. Dan and I were so proud about our precious new child, the long-awaited boon!

In January of 1987, Dan and I attended a leadership conference at which I delivered a prophetic word about a child who was very ill and was expected to die. I exhorted the parents not to worry as their child would live and not die. No one responded to the word. Little did I know that, in a couple of months, Dan and I would be those parents, the recipients of the fulfillment of that word.

We all adored Samuel and enjoyed the months that followed as we cared for him together. His disposition was so good, and we all loved him. The doctors were concerned about his slow weight gain, but other than that, he seemed to be a healthy, normal baby boy. Then, in May of 1987, Samuel developed what appeared to be symptoms of the flu. He began to vomit, but there was no fever. This went on for a couple of days, and I noticed that he seemed to be getting weaker and weaker.

On the afternoon of Thursday, May 7, I put him down for a nap. I was in the middle of redecorating our kitchen and was hanging a piece of wallpaper when I heard God speak to me to go check on Samuel. I tried to argue with God, as I wanted to finish hanging the paper. But the sense got stronger, so I left what I was doing and went upstairs. I was shocked to find Samuel unable to lift his head or stand. I immediately picked him up and carried him to a neighbor who was a nurse. She said that I had to rush him to the doctor, as something indeed was seriously wrong.

The doctor saw him right away and thought at first he might have spinal meningitis but decided to take an X-ray before doing a spinal tap. I took him next door to the radiology office and waited there for the results of the X-rays. Soon a nurse ran up the sidewalk from the pediatrician's office and took my arm. She rushed me back into the doctor's office, and he gave me the news that Samuel was in congestive heart failure. There was an ambulance waiting outside to take us to the hospital, and one of my friends arrived just in time to follow us there. I was in shock. I thought, *This cannot be happening to our son of promise.* Unbeknownst to us at the time, the entire real-life drama that was about to unfold was almost like a dry run for what we faced eleven years later in 1998.

When we arrived at the hospital, there was a bustle of nurses and doctors all around seeking to save our little boy's life. Our pediatrician, Dr. Frank Pedreira, who was a believer and was used in healing ministry, said the situation looked very grave. Dan and I were numb. They called a special ambulance to take Sam to the Georgetown University Hospital to be cared for in their special pediatric intensive care ward. To our great disappointment, they did not let us ride with Samuel in the ambulance, so Dan and I had to follow in our own car.

We were so shaken up, but we knew that we had to be strong and not fall apart. Friends activated the prayer chain, and calls began to go out all over the country. In the car on the way to the hospital, Dan and I knew we had to release Samuel into the LORD's hands. We began to worship, singing the great hymns of suffering saints from long ago. With tears in our eyes, we sang one hymn after another, trying not to panic. Our faith in God's goodness was being challenged, and we had to fight to hold on.

I ran down the hall of Georgetown University Hospital, anxious for news of whether Sam had made it alive. By the time we arrived in his intensive care room, they already had him hooked up to four IVs, one in each limb. He looked so pale and lifeless. They even had an oxygen tent over him. The doctor's report was grim. They said he probably had viral myocarditis, and no medicine could cure it. "His heart is blown up like a balloon," the doctor told us. "The echo-cardiogram ejection fraction test shows almost no pumping action." The medicines they were using were only to strengthen the heart's pumping action by opening the arteries. The walls of the heart were very thin and in danger of bursting. They gave Sam only a 20 percent chance of making it through the night. In fact, we were told, "When a heart is this badly stretched, it does not return to normal. If he is stabilized and survives, he will likely be a bed baby."

Next, we were informed that if he did live, he would have to be in the hospital for at least six weeks. Afterward, if he were lucky to live through the hospital experience, he would need a heart transplant and around-the-clock nursing care. I asked the doctor if he would ever play baseball, and he looked at me kind of oddly and said, "Of course not, his heart is so enlarged that it will never go back to normal." He thought we were in denial and not facing his true condition. We left that evening feeling very distraught.

The next day, we activated a world-wide prayer chain as we had friends who lived in various countries. Many within the Messianic Jewish movement prayed. Additionally, several pastors from the area and elders from our congregation came together to pray in a vacant room near Samuel's. For several hours, we prayed and sought the LORD. A friend encouraged Dan to lay hands on Samuel, to anoint him and declare his healing. So Dan went. I asked God for a sign that Sam would indeed recover. Dan lifted up the oxygen tent, placed his hands on Sam's forehead, and proclaimed his healing. Dan then proceeded to play peek-a-boo with him. Samuel's face lit up into a big smile. This was my sign! Before this, there had been no response to our being in the room, and I was concerned that Sam had lost his winsome personality forever. Perhaps God would heal him after all.

The next day, prophetic words began to come in about people seeing God's hands holding Samuel's heart and shrinking it. One dear friend believed that Samuel would be healed no matter how our faith fluctuated. He would be normal.

Sure enough, the doctor began to wean Samuel off all medications, and God answered my prayers that none of the IVs would have to be replaced. Even though his echocardiogram still showed a damaged heart with little pumping action, all of his external behavior seemed to be returning to normal. Every morning when we would arrive at the hospital, there would be a group of doctors surrounding his bed discussing the anomaly of his condition. In fact, interns lectured on this case, saying this was a case where a patient's clinical condition did not coincide with his behavior; there was no explanation.

During the day when I stayed with Samuel, I often would talk to the other parents who had children in intensive care. Many of them had leukemia and other diseases that I had once feared. Our conversations centered on percentages. What percent chance did our children have of living? It was a dream world—a nightmare, really—that focused on statistics, IVs, lab tests, and beeping life-support systems. I can remember thinking that children with leukemia had a better chance of living than our son and even envied them.

When we left the hospital at night and went out to eat, it seemed that every parent in the restaurant had a son Samuel's age. Our hearts were pierced as we longed to have a normal family again, like they did. I wondered if we would ever be able to bounce our son on our shoulders again.

On a positive note, Samuel seemed to have gained the heart of the nurses and doctors. Many could not keep away from his room. One doctor in particular, who just so happened to have the same birthday as Sam, became especially attached. Often I would find Samuel in his lap. He had to be pulled away from Sam by the nurses so that he could attend to his other duties. God had everything under control; Samuel was given the best medical care.

The doctors released Samuel from the hospital after eight days. They trained each family member in artificial resuscitation because they said that Sam's heart was still paper-thin. He could go into heart failure at any time, we were told. They also told us to expect him to take one step forward and two steps back. They did not expect him to live, as they believed that his heart would never go back to normal; it would always remain enlarged with muscle damage. When I walked out of that hospital before other parents who had seriously ill children, I thought, *Why me and not them?*

During the following weeks and months, we continued to monitor Sam closely and to take him for routine check-ups. Visit after visit to the hospital showed no improvement. Yet the doctors were puzzled. "Does he struggle to empty his bottle?" they would ask.

"No," we answered.

"Does he act lethargic?" they'd then question.

"No, he even climbs up and down the stairs for fun," we replied.

Even so, he took four different kinds of heart medication four times a day. Many times, I battled with Sam to force these medications down only to have him throw them up and the process be repeated. This routine went on for a year and was one of the causes of Sam's struggle with my authority later on; he hated the feeling of being restrained. The other cause was that he had been tied down in the hospital for several days with four IVs, and that I did not spend the nights with him as I had figured that he was too medicated to notice. He feared being controlled. In fact, his doctor said that the reason he resisted eating and potty training was because these were two areas in which he could still be in control.

The other behavior change was anger flare-ups. Before the hospital stay, he was an easy-going child, but afterward he would get so angry that he would kick and bite. What had happened? They said that this was normal too, but we were never able to release him from the effects of the trauma. He continued to be afraid to be alone. Once in a while, something would tap into the buried rage, and he would do something destructive. We did much prayer and fasting for him during the years following, yet these struggles endeared him to our hearts even more. We called him our little lamb.

During Sam's check-ups, the doctors were always amazed: his heart still showed no change, yet he did not get out of breath from eating, climbing stairs, or playing. His activity corresponded to any normal boy of his age. During this season, I was still in a state of shock and expected his every cold or sickness would kill him. Many times, I took him back to the doctor's office, fearing the worst, yet I always came home with a good report.

After six months, Sam's echocardiograms began to show improvement, and after a year, his heart had returned to normal function and size. We were all amazed, including the doctors. The full account of this wonderful miracle was recounted in a booklet called *The Power of God to Heal*. It contains actual copies of medical records and Dr. Pedraira's testimony. Eventually, our Samuel's

miracle story was told on the 700 Club. God must have had a special purpose for sparing his life, we thought.

   God had revealed himself as the God who healed once again!
We were carried along on people's prayers, and though we stumbled, we did not fall headlong. Why God chose to heal Samuel
at this time I do not know. He healed him, even though we as
parents did not have the faith that he would be restored. We had
hope. My battle was not for healing faith but rather against fear.
While I was at the hospital, I spent most of my time in a spare
room seeking God and drawing near to him. I kept reading books
on faith and healing, but knew that I could not work up what it
took to release healing power. Was it a sovereign act of God? Was
it the result of another's faith? A combination? These are still
questions I struggle with today.

Fading Health

He will have no fear of bad news; his heart is steadfast, trusting in the LORD. His heart is secure, he will have no fear; in the end he will look in triumph on his foes.

Psalm 112:7–8

I will be glad and rejoice in your love, for you saw my affliction and knew the anguish of my soul. You have not handed me over to the enemy but have set my feet in a spacious place.

Psalm 31:7–8

Two years after Sam's illness and recovery, we moved from our house of six years to be near the land where we were eventually going to build our congregational facilities. In the process of moving, I came under such stress that it wore down my immune system. It had taken eight months to sell our house. When you have four small children and are trying to keep a perfectly neat house for prospective buyers to view, you approach a near-impossible feat. So many times real estate agents would call ahead and say they were coming over in an hour and then not show up—and this went on for eight months!

Then, we foolishly put a noncontingent contract on a new house we were having built so as not to lose it. We came close to paying the mortgage on two houses at the same time; I almost went over the edge from worry! But God came through at the last minute, and we found a buyer who put down cash with a no-contingency contract. We were able to close on both houses and move in the summer of 1989. Within two weeks of moving, before most of the boxes were unpacked, Dan and I went on a little getaway to the Virgin Islands for a week. Then, after returning, we once again had to pack up and go to a Messianic Jewish conference. By this time, I began to run a fever and have night sweats, but we went anyway. This fever went on for several days, making me weaker and weaker. I could barely function and finally decided to visit the local hospital near the conference center.

After waiting several hours for the test results to come back from my blood work, I felt foolish and got dressed. I thought it was probably just the flu and that I was making a big deal out of nothing. Just as I was about to leave, however, the doctor walked in and said, "Where are you going? You cannot leave. You are in danger of dying!" I couldn't believe it. He said that my blood count was so low (WBC or white blood cell count was 2,200 and the platelets were 60,000, if that means anything to you) that if I bumped myself I would bleed to death internally. I had what they called endocarditis.

They immediately admitted me into the hospital and told me that I must have an intensive program of antibiotics to kill off the bacteria that had attached itself to my heart valve. I would be in the hospital from four to six weeks. I wondered about what would happen to my family.

A prayer chain was activated at the conference, and soon I began to receive visitors. Several leaders came to pray over me, and one leader in particular had a strong sense that I was healed. Still, I did not trust the word and felt like I needed the rest anyway.

Arrangements were made for the children to fly home to be with my parents, and Dan joined them after the conference. They were having a big family reunion, and my children did not want to miss it. After everyone departed, I was left all alone to feel sorry for myself. How could I ever last six weeks, miles away from my family and friends?

That first night, fear tried to take hold of me, but God reassured me through the word that it wasn't my time to die yet. Very clearly, he spoke to my heart and told me to turn to Mark 9:1. I looked it up, not knowing what it said. The words "I tell you the truth, some who are standing here will not taste death before they see the kingdom of God come with power" jumped off the page, and I received encouragement. To this day these words reassure me that I will be alive when the church is moving in victory.

My stay in the hospital did not bring me a sense of closeness with God as did my other hospital stays. I struggled to keep my attitude right and to not fall into watching TV continually. Only a couple of people—for whom I was very grateful—visited me from the local congregation. I spent most of my stay in the hospital alone in bed, hooked up to an IV. The first echocardiogram showed the bacteria growth on my mitral valve, which confirmed the doctor's diagnosis.

After many days, the doctors were unable to isolate the bacteria causing the infection, so they decided to do another echocardiogram. God comforted me through Scripture and seemed to be saying that they would look for it but not be able to find it. And praise the LORD, God did cut off the "enemy," and there was no more growth. My doctor had said that there was no room for God to act, and that even if God did heal me, he would still have to keep me in the hospital for four to six weeks of antibiotic therapy. However, he finally considered sending me to a hospital closer to my home, which greatly encouraged me. But after the last test on the sixth day, he suddenly changed his mind; he told me he was taking me off all medications in two days and that I could go home. How amazing to see the doctors change their "absolute" plans! What appeared to be an immovable obstacle, a prison sentence with no way out, became nothing in the hands of an all-powerful God. God opened the door, and the prisoner went free! God is so good. He made me lie down in green pastures and led me beside still waters. I did not experience any fireworks, just the peaceful realization that God heals the "broken hearted." What Satan had meant for evil, God had meant for good.

Light Obscured

And the boy Samuel continued to grow in stature and in favor with the LORD and with men.

1 Samuel 2:26

Samuel, in his younger years, loved to worship. He often would get prophetic words during the service that would be a confirmation of Dan's sermon. It presented some difficulty for me because he would get proud, and sometimes I had to restrain him from giving the word. This did not make him too happy.

He gave words at other times too. One time, he was playing in our house and running around like a little boy when he suddenly stopped and jumped up on a chair. He then began to prophesy over one of our boarders about a particular health problem she was having, saying she would get better if I prayed over her every morning and night. After finishing, he jumped back down off the chair and went back to playing.

Samuel loved God, but sometimes, when we were in a particularly anointed time of worship, I would sense oppression come over him, even when he was still a toddler. This especially happened after he was baptized at age six. We baptized him at a young age because he said an angel told him to do it. He said that he often saw angels, but after he was baptized, the battle over his spiritual heart intensified. It became more difficult for him to worship. In the natural, we had to battle over his physical heart, but then we had to battle over his spiritual heart. The enemy knew that this was a special child, and he took every opportunity to attack him.

For many years, we would put him to bed only to find him sleeping on the floor in the hallway next to our room or in one of the other siblings' rooms. Often, we would find him sleeping half in and half out of his room on the floor. He was very adamant about not sleeping alone. Sometimes, I would let him sleep in our room on the floor when Dan was out of town. The other children were very tolerant of his nomadic behavior as well. We called him our wandering Jew and sensed that perhaps this was preparation for his world travel someday. He often was plagued with nightmares about dying. Even though he was the recipient of much prayer from powerful, well-known men and women of God, for some reason God chose not to deliver him from his fears. To this day, I still don't know why. God often does not tell us why.

Samuel found obedience difficult and sometimes even intolerable. He loved life and all sorts of fun but seemed to lack self-control, even though he showed such spiritual sensitivity. Being denied what he wanted led to tantrums at times. As I said before, we questioned whether or not his fear of sleeping alone and his difficulty with obedience were related to the ordeal of his near-death experience.

In the midst of his own personal struggle, however, his love of life was something beautiful to behold for us as his parents. He loved sports and he excelled in physical coordination. He could do anything he put his mind to. Samuel played tennis, basketball, and volleyball. He did rollerblading, swimming, skiing, bicycling, hiking, and fishing. He loved life and did not want to miss out on even one minute of it. He did not even want to take time to change his clothes into pajamas at night because it cut short his fun. Even when we took him skiing for the first time, he picked it up so quickly that by the second day he was fearlessly "shooshing" down intermediate slopes.

He showed the same type of ability when he was old enough to learn to ride a bicycle. Dan held the back of the bike as he had done with each child before Samuel. He did this so he could run down the street and stabilize the bike for them. Then, after many dry runs, he would finally let the child try alone. But not with Sam. On the first run he told his father to let go, and he took off down the road like a seasoned pro.

He had such a zest for life. I remember him jumping out of tall trees without getting hurt. He loved to walk his dog while he was rollerblading and to let the dog run swiftly ahead of him, pulling him at lightning speed. He even excelled in gymnastics. I loved watching him as he tirelessly tried each move over and over again to get it down perfectly. The instructors loved to work with him because he was fearless. It brought me so much joy to see him come alive as he twisted and turned his body to do amazing feats. I asked myself numerous times, "How could this fearless child be so fearful at night?"

Because of Sam's high energy level and perfectionism, he would get behavior marks at school; not many of them, just enough to discourage him and bring down his self-esteem. Even though every teacher adored him because of his spontaneity and love, he presented a challenge to them. By the end of fifth grade, he begged to be home-schooled. After much prayer, we thought that this was best for him. We had home-schooled Simcha for her sixth-grade year to prepare her for her bat mitzvah, so we decided to give Sam the same opportunity.

The week before I started to home-school, Dan and I took Samuel up in front of our congregational sanctuary after services and prophesied over him. I told him that before he reached his thirteenth birthday (his bar mitzvah), he would love obedience. We had him hold the Torah scroll, and I told him that God's Word would be his delight and that the struggle he was having with the enemy would soon be over. He loved these encouraging words, as he knew that his battle was not against flesh and blood. In the midst of some of the most intense conflicts in his younger years, he would always encourage me by saying, "Remember the dream, Mommy [the one I had before he was conceived]. God will make everything all right."

Looking back on this, I thank God for this gift of spending Sam's last year in such a close way. We loved being together, and he even wanted to be home-schooled for his seventh-grade year, too. Since he was not bound to regular school hours, we were able to take him on several ministry trips with us. He really enjoyed this quality time together, and we noticed that gradually his heart grew more and more tender. He became quick to obey and even rededicated his life to God during a trip to Pensacola. I can still see him dancing with abandonment before the LORD. Two songs in particular became his favorite at these meetings, and they were sung at his resurrection service.

In this last year, Dan and I not only decided to home-school Samuel, but we also chose to buy him a golden Labrador retriever. Sam and his wonderful dog slept together, helping to relieve Sam's fears about sleeping alone. During this time, Sam was having a different struggle—a struggle deciding between becoming an Olympic gymnast or a Baltimore Orioles player. Baseball was his father's first love, so sometimes Samuel would withdraw from his interest in baseball as his way of rebelling against his father. But, during the last month of his life, he forsook gymnastics and knew that he most wanted to become a baseball star—that was his dream. Also, a young man in our congregation took a special interest in Samuel and became his personal coach. Samuel adored Chad (our future son-in-law) and took to copying everything he did. He would practice for hours the exercises Chad gave him to do, and he hounded us daily to pitch balls to him or to play catch. We were winning his heart. Even though he knew that one day he would preach the Gospel, he thought that playing baseball would not be a diversion.

We loved to watch him play baseball. I can remember watching his first game when he was eight years old. The words came back to us that the doctor had said in the hospital about Samuel never being able to play baseball. Dan and I both wept. God had proven the doctor wrong!

Not only was Sam gifted athletically and prophetically, but he was gifted evangelistically. He loved to tell others about Yeshua. He did not care if they were black or white, adult or child; he wanted them to know God. He had a profound effect on some of the children in the neighborhood. In fact, one of his childhood friends was actively involved in our youth group for a time; I believe it was because of Sam. I know he influenced others.

Faint Foreshadowing

After he was weaned, she took the boy with her, young as he was ... and brought the boy to Eli, and she said to him, "As surely as you live, my LORD, I am the woman who stood here beside you praying to the LORD. I prayed for this child, and the LORD has granted me what I asked of him. So now I give him to the LORD. For his whole life he will be given over to the LORD." And he worshiped the LORD there.

1 Samuel 1:24–28

The boy Samuel ministered before the LORD under Eli. In those days the word of the LORD was rare; there were not many visions. One night Eli, whose eyes were becoming so weak that he could barely see, was lying down in his usual place. The lamp of God had not yet gone out, and Samuel was lying down in the temple of the LORD, where the ark of God was. Then the LORD called Samuel. Samuel answered, "Here I am."

1 Samuel 3:1–4

On Saturday, June 6, 1998, we celebrated our daughter Simcha's bat mitzvah. My father and mother came, along with my sister, Lorie, and her two girls, Jessica and Alycia. My mother was weak from fighting pancreatic cancer, but she did not want to miss this special occasion. Dan's sister, Joyce, and her husband, Ed, also came.

Everyone was at our house for a picnic after services. While many ate and played volleyball, I sat in a lawn chair among a circle of my friends. We discussed the upcoming trip that my older two children, Ben, age twenty-three, and Becca, age twenty-one, were taking to Ethiopia. One lady asked me if I was worried about their safety since there was war going on in the northern part of the country. I said, "No, I do not worry about my children dying because life and death are in the hands of God. What I do worry about are finances because I feel like it is my fault when there isn't enough money. I am the one who writes the checks and spends most of the money." Little did I know that my words would be tested a week later, and little did our relatives know that this would be their final good-bye to Samuel.

Ben and Becca left for Ethiopia on Tuesday night. Samuel, Simcha, and I went to a good-bye party that night for them and the other members of the team going on the trip. Several members of our congregation also came to send them off, and we spent a considerable amount of time praying for them. Ben and others had quite a strong sense that they were going to learn and experience a greater depth of intercession. I knew they would never be the same again. Then, there was Sam, who was so bored and not too happy about attending. But at least he got a chance to hug his big brother and sister before they left.

During the remainder of the week, I woke up with gratefulness in my heart. I kept looking at the beauty of nature, my surroundings, my family, and my home with the sense that the Lord was speaking to me, "Take a good look, take everything in, because soon life will never be the same for you." Although I had this sense, little did I know that everything we were to experience with Samuel would be our last encounters with him.

I specifically remember our last baseball game. It was a colder than usual June night, and the weather was slightly drizzly, gray, and bleak. Dan had driven back from Richmond, where he was speaking at Youth with a Mission School of Jewish Studies all week. Originally, he was going to stay in Richmond until Saturday afternoon because he had to speak at one of our Tikkun congregations, but Sam and I urged him to come home Thursday night since he did not have to speak anywhere on Friday. We praise God for the decisions we made to spend more time with Sam during the last few days and months of his life.

Samuel took his friend Karl (our beloved neighbor who would be in the fire with Sam) to watch him play that night. Unfortunately, Sam wasn't playing his best and made several mistakes, which Dan tried to correct. Of course, Sam did not appreciate that because he thought his dad was not as knowledgeable about baseball as was Chad, his personal coach. But Dan discussed the game with Sam afterward anyway and took him to Seven-Eleven, his favorite post-game hangout. Samuel and I then played Rummikub together. I think we each won a game.

Then, there was our last Shabbat meal together, and I still remember how great the steak tasted that night. Samuel asked for the most tender piece of steak, and of course, Dan gave it to him. I recollect jokingly remarking, "What about me, don't I deserve a tender piece too?" After dinner, we participated in our usual family time and prayed and worshiped together. Dan blessed everyone who was present and gave a special blessing to Sam, who was sitting on his lap. He prayed long life and protection over him while Sam snuggled deep within his arms. They had a special evening planned and hastily went down to our recreation room to watch the Chicago Bulls beat Utah in a playoff. I went to bed.

The next morning, Dan returned to Richmond to speak while I took Simcha and Sam to our services. Samuel was unusually attentive during the worship service. His usual agitation was gone that morning. Several members gave prophetic words that day, including me. Someone prophesied about not looking at circumstances, and I confirmed it by adding that you cannot let circumstances tempt you to believe that God does not love you. I quoted from Romans 8 about how nothing will separate us from the love of God—"not death, nor life, neither angels nor demons, neither the present nor the future, nor any powers ... nor trouble or hardship or persecution or famine or nakedness or danger or sword." Also, I recounted the teaching I gave at our intercessory class about the importance of hearing God's voice and not letting our hearts become hardened like King Saul's. Through his rejection of hearing God's word on two different occasions (first, when Samuel told him to wait for him before sacrificing and he didn't; and second, when he did not completely destroy the Amalekites like he was told to do), Saul could no longer hear God since God was not speaking to him. Out of desperation, he went to a witch to get a supernatural word when he was threatened by the Philistines. "Today, if you hear his voice, do not harden your heart" (Hebrews 3:7).

Another man got up and exhorted us to be bold in our witness. He compared boldness with a person pounding on a door to get people out of a building on fire in an attempt to rescue them. How much more should we be concerned about the lives going to the eternal fire? He talked about the recent Beth Messiah men's retreat (a weekend of teaching and spiritual renewal) and how it was a breakthrough for men, getting them out of passivity. There was much retaliation after the retreat in the form of physical injury and relational conflicts between leaders. We were exhorted to be on guard and not to flag in zeal.

Ron Cantor, our college and career leader, then gave a teaching about spiritual warfare and closed the message with an altar call for all men age thirteen and over who wanted to be warriors in the kingdom to come forward. Samuel, who was only twelve, wanted so badly to go forward. He seemed so different that morning and hung onto every word Ron preached. I did not let him go forward, but as I look back on it, I wish I had.

That Saturday was special in another way for Samuel, as he was released to finally join the youth group. His sister put up a fuss at first, as she thought that Sam was too young, but she made peace and was happy to have her younger brother join the group.

On the way home and into the afternoon, there continued to be conflicts between different members of the household and Sam. It had started out that morning with a conflict between a boarder and Sam, then between him and his sister, then a conflict with me over walking the dog, and finally with his father over letting Butter run through the mud puddles in the back of our house. It seemed that that Saturday there was clearly a battle between good and evil over Sam's life; it was almost like he was ready to take off into the things of God, and Satan was trying desperately to stop him.

In the middle of all these conflicts, Sam began to have one of his pity parties and remarked quite adamantly that he deserved to die. By this time, I was burned out by all the conflicts and was fighting a spirit of hopelessness. I despairingly wondered if these conflicts over Samuel's life would ever be over.

In January, I had prayed and fasted two weeks for his spiritual heart. Just when we were making progress, it looked like we stumbled backwards. Usually, I would come sharply against such statements like the one he made that Saturday and have him rebuke and renounce his words. I would then make him speak a pronouncement of life over himself, but I failed to do so at that particular time. All I managed to say was, "That's right, Sam, you do deserve to die, and so do I and so does everyone else; that is why Yeshua came to die for us, so we would not have to die." I chose to ignore the black cloud that appeared to enter him when he spoke these curses because, within a short period of time, he sprang back to life. Sam and his father reconciled, and it wasn't long before he convinced his father to go to the sports store that afternoon, after failing to get a "yes" out of me. He wanted to spend some of the money he had earned digging out bushes in our front yard.

Sam had informed Dan that his batting gloves were torn. The next day would be his last game of Little League season. The Sabbath was not yet over, and though Dan was tired and protested going, compassion overtook him. He told Sam to call the store to see if it was open since there was a power outage. If the store was open, he agreed to take him. After 5 p.m., the two of them left. They would have to be quick about it, seeing as Dan had a meeting at 6:30 p.m.

On the way over to the store, Dan was listening to a tape with headphones on.

Sam asked, "Are you going to listen to that in the store?"

Dan smiled and said to Sam, "Oh, Sam, you want to spend time with me, don't you?"

"Yes, Daddy," he said as his face lit up. Both father and son shared a memorable moment as they hugged.

Dan and Sam entered the store and first looked at bats. Sam tried to get his father to buy one that was worth over $150. Sam assured his father it would make him a much better hitter. Somehow, Dan negotiated his way away from the bats and to the gloves. Sam's expensive taste led him to the $19 Nike gloves. Already, Sam had picked up a $10 major league baseball, making his total purchase over the $20 he had to spend. As they walked toward the checkout, Sam noticed a bin of cheaper baseballs. "You know, Dad, I really think I should get four of these instead. It costs less, and it is better to have more balls since Chad pitches several balls to me," Sam said. Dan agreed.

At the checkout, Dan saw Sam open up his wallet, disclosing only the $20 bill. Suddenly full of compassion for his son once again, Dan agreed to pay for the balls after Sam promised to pay him back. Dan would hear nothing of it; he told Sam that this was as much for himself as it was for him. It was his joy to watch his son play baseball!

When Sam and Dan got back from the store, I was sitting in our pink chair, relaxing and getting myself mentally ready to rush off to our monthly Messianic Council Meeting, a gathering of Tikkun pastors who met regularly for mutual encouragement and equipping. Sam jumped over the chair sideways to end up in my lap. He hugged me with such excitement as he showed me his new purchases. Still hurting from all the conflicts of the day, I was not in a very good mood and did not fully hug him back as I usually do. If only I had known that this was to be his last hug.

When we left for the meeting, Simcha and her friend Hannah remained at home while Sam went out to play at his friend's house next door. A severe storm had just swept through the area, and that was why the power had been knocked out. I did not worry about it too much because I felt certain that the electricity would be restored soon. Our council meeting went well, but during the worship, the spirit highlighted a scripture to me.

> And the LORD said to Moses, "When you return to Egypt, see that you perform before Pharaoh all the wonders I have given you the power to do. But I will harden his heart so that he will not let the people go. Then say to Pharaoh, 'This is what the LORD says: Israel is my firstborn son, and I told you, "Let my son go, so he may worship me." But you refused to let him go; so I will kill your firstborn son.'"
>
> Exodus 4:21–23

I pondered this in my heart and continued trying to pay attention to the worship and teaching time. We had lights where we were meeting, but I was still a little apprehensive about our children at home; I was unsure of their current power situation, so I called them. Simcha said that they still did not have electricity but that she was having a good time with her friend. She also said that Sam and his friends were playing games with them. At one point she got a little frightened, so she and Hannah walked through the neighborhood worshiping the LORD. Knowing that Simcha had pleasant memories of her last moments with Samuel helped me comfort Simcha in her grief later.

We got home a little after 11:30 p.m. and found that Sam had gone to stay at the neighbor's house, at the Carmans,' overnight. Charles and Katie Carman were a couple with a thirteen- and eleven-year-old who were especially close to our Sam. They were having a sleepover, Simcha said, and he just went over there without waiting for permission. He told one of our boarders where he was going (however, she was not in charge of him and bore no responsibility). When she asked him if he had our approval, he told her we wouldn't mind, so she let him go. When we found out, we were a little fearful, as the power had not come back on yet. We still had many candles burning, so I went around blowing them out and told Simcha to blow hers out before going to bed.

I can remember looking out her window at the neighbor's house and wondering whether I should check to see if they had blown out their candles. I couldn't discern if that was the Holy Spirit prompting me or just a mother's tendency to be overly concerned. After hesitating a few moments, I made a conscious choice to trust God and the maturity of the parents next door to oversee the children. I had such a sense of placing Samuel in God's hands. Later, this helped me to understand that I wasn't even a victim of God. God did not "take" Samuel from me, as I had "placed" him voluntarily into his hands.

Before bed, Dan began to express his concern quite strongly, and I asked him if he sensed any danger. He said he didn't think so. He was just bothered by the fact that Sam did not get permission to spend the night. After thinking about it for a few minutes, he said that Sam would probably have fun and that he didn't see any harm in letting him remain with his friends.

In the middle of the night, I was awakened with a physical attack of pain in my body, so I spent time praying for my children in Ethiopia and other things the LORD brought to mind. I tried to sense if anyone was in need of special prayer, but I heard nothing. After about a half hour, I went back to sleep. We were awakened at 5:15 a.m. with our neighbor pounding at the door yelling, "Fire, fire!"

Quickly, Dan and I got dressed. We were totally disoriented because it was still dark; the electricity was still out. It was awkward to pick out clothes in the dark (I ended up with mismatched hot pink pants and top), and then I was too frantic to put shoes on. What warranted such an abrupt awakening?

Fire! Fire!

The sinners in Zion are terrified; trembling grips the godless:
"Who of us can dwell with the consuming fire? Who of us can
dwell with everlasting burning?"

Isaiah 33:14

The LORD said to Satan, "The LORD rebuke you, Satan! The
LORD, who has chosen Jerusalem, rebuke you! Is not this man a
burning stick snatched from the fire?"

Zechariah 3:2

Katrine, one of our boarders; Dan; and I rushed downstairs and out our front door, apprehensive about the extent of the crisis we were facing. As I bounded off our front step, I immediately turned left toward the house where Sam was sleeping. Wet mud oozed through my bare toes as I almost slipped down the slope between our houses. We were shocked by the extent of smoke and fire pouring out the side window of the basement. This did not look good. Our neighbor Charles, who was frantically running toward us, told us that his children and Sam were still trapped in the basement.

Charles was beside himself with panic and screamed, "I'm sorry. I'm so sorry!" He was grabbing his head in his hands and wildly mentioned that he was only able to get one of his sons out and that his oldest was still in the doorway. The teenager was too heavy for one man to lift him up over the glass from the broken French door. Apparently, Charles first tried to use his head to break the window but then saw a cement splash block and ended up using that to break in. He had made several trips into the house in an attempt to rescue the boys, but he was unable to locate them because of all the thick, black smoke. Later, we found out that he even put grass in his mouth to try to filter out the smoke when he breathed.

Dan tried to ascertain from him where the boys were located in the basement so that he could go in and rescue them, but Charles was incoherent. In the meantime, I ran around the back and tried to assess the situation for myself. I found one of Sam's friends on the ground in the backyard. He labored for every breath that he took, and his chest extended grotesquely with each gasp of air.

Then, I came face to face with the broken glass door in the back wall of the walkout basement. Shattered glass lay all around

Refined by Fire

the doorway, both inside and out. There lay Charles's older son with one of his arms draped over the broken glass door. As we were waiting for the other neighbors to come and help, I decided to try to lift Joe from the doorway by myself. Without much thought as to the consequences, I proceeded to walk carefully over the broken glass in my bare feet.

Inside the burning house, the smoke was so overpowering that even one breath of it was deadly. The fire had spread out over the back of the recreation room and was already out of control. Some flames even raged up the stairwell to the first floor. It was so hot that the fixtures in the bathroom and on the sliding door had melted. I attempted to lift the boy but could not budge him. If only I could reach Samuel, but there was too much thick, dark smoke for me to see through, and I couldn't keep holding my breath. Sam was close, yet he might as well have been miles away; I could not go to him. I kept yelling for someone to do something, but we were all in a state of shock.

Eventually, Dan and a neighbor lifted the teenager out of the doorway, but they were not able to go back in. No one seemed to be able to tell us where the boys were sleeping. Dan and I thought they were sleeping in the farthest back bedroom but later found out that they were sleeping in the bedroom just ten feet from where we were standing.

At that point, we had two boys lying on the ground near the back white rail fence. Their backs arched as they struggled for each breath. I sensed the terror in their soot-covered faces and could only imagine the horror they had just experienced. Later, I learned that they had been sleeping in the back bedroom when they were awakened by smoke and the screams coming from the other three boys, Samuel, Karl (the eleven-year-old son of Charles), and Matt, another twelve-year-old friend of Karl who was spending the night. The two boys broke down the door separating the two rooms and then tried to rescue the other boys. Within a few seconds, the suffocating smoke overcame them, and they collapsed on the floor

123

near the exit. They had tried to open the back basement door, but the door fixtures were too hot to handle.

(In later inquiries it was discovered that the boys were up playing Monopoly by candlelight until about 1:30 a.m., when Samuel, Karl, and Matt went to bed. Brad and Joe stayed up for a couple more hours. Joe finally went to bed at about 4:30 a.m. He blew out all the candles except one, a tapered candle sitting on the shelf of an end unit in the back of the recreation room. He thought it would be safe as it had burned down quite a bit, and he figured it would go out by itself. Somehow, in that short forty-five minute period between the time when he said he went to bed and the time we were awakened, a raging fire grew out of that small candle that had fallen to the carpet.)

Frantically, I ran out of the basement and went between Charles and Dan, begging them to do something. Couldn't they go in and rescue Sam and the other boys? There seemed to be such confusion. It almost seemed like we were being prevented from going into the fiery inferno.

As the minutes ticked by, the flames continued to lap up everything in their path. I fell to the ground outside the broken glass door and knew from that moment on that there was no hope for Samuel's survival. "Samuel! Samuel!" I cried. Sam was gone, just like that, and there was nothing I could do. "Oh, God, no!" It was almost like I felt his spirit leave. I kept calling out his name, but it was to no avail.

It felt like forever waiting for the firemen to come. Oh, the stench, the heat, the confusion, the horror. The agony of not knowing intensified. Katrine came over to hug me and exhorted me very strongly to get up and start ministering to the other people. She said that there was nothing I could do for Samuel. Katie Carman had jumped out of the second-story window and had broken her back. Both she and her husband, who was beside himself with guilt and shock, needed prayer. Somehow I found the courage to get up off the ground. The peace and strength of God came into me, and

I was able to start ministering. He took away almost all my fear. I experienced being encapsulated in his arms of love.

Several policemen arrived first. Then came the long procession of fire truck after fire truck with sirens blaring. The crew arrived about ten minutes after they were called, and I was puzzled by why they did not come sooner. It turned out they were on another call, and then, there were those terrible speed bumps—four in all—which slowed down the trucks a few seconds. Every second felt like an eternity. Ambulances began showing up, and our neighborhood became a three-ring circus as firemen threw masses of hoses around, towing them through every available door. Windows began to shatter as the firemen wielded their axes with great urgency. Everything got so confusing from then on that I couldn't remember until later the sequence of what happened.

A fireman brought out a child, but it wasn't Samuel. Later, he recounted that it is usually very difficult to find a fire victim because of the intense smoke. No light can penetrate it. But this time was different, he said; it felt as if he had divine guidance and somehow knew exactly where each child was. Karl, who was unconscious and not breathing, was the first child to be brought out. It didn't look good. A fireman immediately began artificial resuscitation on him. I went inside our house, got on the phone, and activated our prayer chain, telling my friends about the fire and that I did not think Sam was alive. It was about 5:30 a.m. While I was in the house, the fireman drenched himself with water from our garden hose and immediately ran back into the house as another fireman backed him up with a fire extinguisher. This time, the basement flashed over, and the fireman sustained some third-degree burns. Ignoring the pain and danger, he returned to the bedroom and went directly to where Samuel was sleeping. He slung him under his arms and protected his head from the blast of heat. Even though he did not come in direct contact with the flames, little Samuel still received burns over sixty percent of his body.

When I came out of our house, I saw Sam on the ground unconscious with a policeman and a medic working on him. I ran over to where he was lying and started praying and screaming, "Life, in Jesus's name!" over him and rebuking death. I grabbed hold of his ankle. It did not look like he had sustained any burns, as his skin wasn't black and his clothes were not charred. The policeman kept trying to get Dan and me to stand back. I became angry and thought, *Doesn't he still belong to us, and don't we have a right to hold him?*

While Sam was being worked on, someone yelled that there was another child still left inside the basement. Another fireman went in after him and came out in a few seconds with Matt. He wasn't breathing either, and we prayed for him. All five boys had now been rescued from the burning house. Two were breathing without assistance, and the other three were being resuscitated. Karl began to revive and so did Sam, but Matt was never resuscitated.

By this time, the other parents (the birth mom of Charles's three boys and Matt's parents) were arriving as were several reporters. Simcha had awakened because of the noise and discovered what had happened. She began to lose it and wailed uncontrollably. I tried to comfort her and quickly put her to work packing my bag for the hospital. By God's grace, she pulled herself together and became a great support throughout the rest of the ordeal. Also, Eun Young, our other boarder, woke up and began to intercede for what was going on outside. Dan, Katrine, and I huddled in a circle on the sidewalk behind the house. We stood together with our hands tightly intertwined. We released Sam into God's hands and began to worship—anything to keep from getting into fear. We sang the old hymn that had brought us comfort so many years ago, "Be Still My Soul." How this reminded us of the time eleven years before when we fought for Sam's life and God had miraculously healed him. We couldn't believe that we were facing a battle for his life once again. I pled with God, "Didn't we pass the first time?"

One by one, the boys were taken by ambulance to the nearby park and airlifted by the Medivac helicopter to Children's Hospital. I was bothered by the delay and wondered why they weren't taking Samuel to the hospital yet. At one point, I went over to Matt's mom, who was standing with a few of our other neighbors, and told her that God would not let any of the children die; her son was going to be all right. Quite some time passed before Sam stabilized enough to be transported to Shady Grove Hospital. The paramedics were waiting for instructions on where to take him. In the meantime, a policeman asked us for information about Samuel and tried to reassure us that they were doing their best to speed things up. Eventually, they decided to take him by ambulance to Shady Grove first and then airlift him to Children's Hospital in Washington, D.C. We were not allowed to ride with Samuel, so, once again, we had to follow in our own car—just a foretaste of the separation we were about to experience.

Piercing the Darkness

Come, let us return to the LORD. He has torn us to pieces but he will heal us; he has injured us but he will bind up our wounds. After two days he will revive us; on the third day he will restore us, that we may live in his presence. Let us acknowledge the LORD; let us press on to acknowledge him. As surely as the sun rises, he will appear; he will come to us like the winter rains, like the spring rains that water the earth.

Hosea 6:1–3

Simcha gave me my packed bag and a neighbor ran into our house to get my purse and Bible. By this time, one of our elders came to our house. My heart leapt within me as I began to realize that the troops were beginning to rally behind us and that we were not alone. It was such a comfort.

Soon we were on our way and carefully maneuvered our car between the fire trucks, hoses, emergency vehicles, and reporters. Before the ambulances even left our street, the Beth Messiah Congregation prayer chain had been activated. The wife of our associate senior leader was already busy building our network of prayer support through Beth Messiah and our Tikkun-related congregations.

In the car, Dan and I continued to worship God and release Sam into his hands. I was plagued with thoughts of whether or not Sam would still be alive by the time we arrived at Shady Grove Hospital. As soon as we arrived, we rushed into the emergency room. The first person Dan saw was Matt Connor, Sr., the father of young Matt. His son was pronounced dead at Shady Grove. Dan and Matt Sr. embraced and wept together. A nurse immediately escorted us to a separate room where Dan and I could be alone. There we waited to see Samuel.

Several minutes went by, and then we were allowed to see Sam briefly… yes, he was still breathing! The doctors informed us at that time about the extent of Sam's burns. I couldn't believe it because he did not appear burned when they pulled him out of the burning house. But then I lifted the covers and saw several places where his skin was falling off his arms and legs. His little body was completely stripped of his clothing, and he looked so helpless. His ears were badly burned and were beginning to bleed. They said there was blood in his urine, which was normal in these situations. They explained the heat burned his respiratory system and his other vital organs. They tried to sound hopeful.

After Sam was assessed and treated at Shady Grove Hospital, he was transported by Medivac helicopter to Children's Hospital to join the other burn victims. He wasn't expected to live, yet we reasoned that the odds against his living had been great before and we had won the battle for his life then. There was a great possibility we could win this battle, especially since they were able to resuscitate him.

Out in the hall of the hospital, Matt's mother, father, and the father's girlfriend (Matt's parents were divorced) were embracing one another and weeping. Matt was dead. We came over to them and hugged them, giving them our condolences. We felt blessed to have our son still alive yet identified with the grief and shock they were experiencing.

We arrived at Children's Hospital by 8:30 a.m. It seemed like days had already passed, even though it was only a few hours. The first friends to arrive were a dear pastoral couple who had left their church service and came directly to the hospital. By this time, a well-organized prayer alert was sent out all over the world, and numerous volunteers manned phones at our offices for several days, answering the questions of concerned callers.

At the hospital, we were eventually given a whole vacant wing, as many friends from Beth Messiah and other congregations began to gather and watch with us. There were from forty to eighty people with us at all times during our forty-eight-hour vigil. Samuel was on life support in intensive care, and we all took turns standing by his bed, praying and reading scripture over him. He looked so peaceful. I was comforted with the thought that perhaps he did not feel anything when he was burned because it was possible he had already passed out from the toxic smoke.

When I would visit him in the Intensive Care Unit (ICU), I prayed over him and sang. But he did not respond. I told his nurse about his first healing and how God was going to heal him again. I noticed that they had not wrapped his burns yet, and I admonished his nurse to treat him as though he was going to live. They had him on a respirator, and eventually they did wrap him in bandages from head to toe. He looked like a mummy.

After a few hours, the doctor reported that Sam was brain dead and that normally they would immediately disconnect him from life-support, but due to our pleading (and supernatural intervention), they allowed him to stay on it for two days. During this time, Dan and I were so weak that we could not be left alone. Our good friends Michael and Patricia Bryan stayed with us continuously. They would play a pivotal coordinating role for prayer. Besides networking with Tikkun for prayer, Dan asked Michael to see that key churches were called.

We could not sleep. How kind the staff was in letting us use hospital beds to rest. It is a mystery why God had us keep standing for Sam's healing. He could have allowed Sam to die right away, like Matt. For some reason, we were called upon to bear up in faith and not release our grief. Many ministers from all over the world encouraged us to believe for a miracle. Hence, the hospital ward became a hub of massive communication, an international prayer mobilization center, with cell phones, fax machines, and laptop computers. Prayer requests went all over the world within a matter of hours. The Holy Spirit stirred up thousands of believers to pray; many of them did not even know us. Whole churches committed themselves to all-night prayer meetings and to fasting. We kept getting encouraging e-mails and faxes from people who were upholding us in prayer and hearing things from the Lord.

Dan found himself playing the role of a commander over a major military endeavor; only the grace of God sustained him. This was a time of spiritual warfare that had much greater implications, we felt. Here was a show of unity, a cry of the heart from churches around the world and from a representation of churches from our county and country. We had representation from different denominations and streams. The body of Messiah was functioning as it was meant to function. Here was a practical unity of Messianic Jews and Gentiles crying out to God.

However, on the morning we were to disconnect Samuel from his life support system, Dan became ill and lay on the tile floor. Several of the men came over and surrounded him. Soon, I came and lay down next to him. Our friends began to comfort us and to pray fervently for us. Dan was trying to get up the courage to go into the ICU and pray one more time before disconnecting Samuel. One time, I can remember crying as I looked into the faces of our friends and realized that we had it better than Yeshua during his Garden of Gethsemane experience. He could not get a few disciples to wait with him for one hour, but we had almost eighty people watching and waiting with us in the hospital (perhaps thousands elsewhere) during our darkest hour.

The time had finally come. Several of our closest friends went to be by Sam's bedside and support Dan while he pulled the plug. By this time, Sam's little head had swollen to almost twice its size, and his lips were cracked and largely protruding over the tube in his throat. Discolored secretions oozed from his mouth and nose. His body even began to stink. This couldn't be my little boy who just a few days ago had jumped into my lap. The nurse kept pressuring us to hurry up and disconnect him. I was bothered by how they seemed so insensitive. Surely they did not know how much I loved this little boy! There were other children that needed his bed, she said. How strange that Sam belonged to us until he died; then the state "owned" him. I wanted to take him into my arms but could not. As soon as Dan disconnected Sam, I ran out past the nurse and past all the other suffering children. That "run" began days and weeks of "running" in an attempt to find a place of peace.

Though I was upset over this apparent coldness from the nurses toward the end, I must relate how gracious they were in "bending" the rules. Normally, no one besides the immediate family was allowed into the ICU, yet they permitted several of our friends to stay by Sam's side several times. Often, there would be five to eight people at once—highly unusual. Also, they normally did not allow people other than the family to spend the night in the hospital, but they allowed all those present to stay by our side. And, whoever heard of a hospital giving an entire ward over to praying, singing, dancing warriors?

When we went back a few days later to visit Karl, who was still in the hospital and would remain there for several months, they had strictly reinstated the rules with an iron hand. Though this time in the hospital challenged us to the depths of our ability to endure, I found that God's grace was abundant. We did not know why God was having us fight so hard for Sam's resurrection, and why he did not allow us to grieve until after Sam was buried. Yet many upheld us both physically and spiritually through their prayers. People were connecting this battle for Sam's life with God's desire to breathe life into the dry bones of the Jewish people. So when they prayed for Samuel, they prayed for Israel.

One of our leaders in Israel said to keep Sam on life-support as long as we could, as it was keeping prayer going. He noticed a change in the atmosphere over Israel. Truly, something beyond our understanding was taking place. We later received reports of how major breakthroughs among the Orthodox Jews and native Israelis were beginning to happen. There was a new openness to hear the gospel, and many were getting saved. Did Samuel's death and resultant prayers have anything to do with these victories? I do not know, but it feels good to believe it. We were caught up in a drama we did not write and played parts for which we did not audition.

While we were battling in the hospital, our older two children found out about their brother, and they learned intercession at a much deeper level—just as they thought they would before they left the states. The group in Ethiopia—along with several Ethiopians—spent several days and nights praying for Sam's life. The prayers were intense and extended. Our children were convinced that he would live and not die. When they found out that he was taken off life support, they were devastated. Several friends offered to pay for their trip back to the states so that they could attend his funeral. Yet they believed that God was calling them to stay in Ethiopia rather than to come home. This decision proved very difficult for them, but we supported them. It may be several years, unless God comes through, for them to enter into a spiritual battle again for someone's life like they did for Samuel's life. I have to trust God to heal their wounds of running into that "brick wall" as I had in 1989.

Those who heard accurately from the Lord were in agreement. None said that Sam would be resurrected, but all said that we should stand for his resurrection. We will probably never completely understand why God chose this path for us to take, but may he continue to receive glory through our obedience during those difficult times.

The Twinkling of an Eye

Listen, I tell you a mystery: We will not all sleep, but we will all be changed—in a flash, in the twinkling of an eye, at the last trumpet. For the trumpet will sound, the dead will be raised imperishable, and we will be changed. For the perishable must clothe itself with the imperishable, and the mortal with immortality. When the perishable has been clothed with the imperishable, and the mortal with immortality, then the saying that is written will come true: "Death has been swallowed up in victory."

1 Corinthians 15:51–54

I went to the funeral (we called it Sam's resurrection service) still feeling suspended—somewhere between heaven and hell, I believe. The hordes of hell and grief were pressing in on my spirit, yet my body's natural "novocain" was numbing me. I guess this numbing was the gift of God for me to be able to go through the tragedy. A surrealistic movie played out before my eyes; it was as if I was somehow a real character patched onto a backdrop of cartoon characters and events. No way can what I was experiencing have been real; it did not compute. Years before my mother had gone through the same pain, and her son never returned. He remained dead the next day, the day after that, and the day after that. Never did she wake from her nightmare. In the same way, I was destined to live out the same horrible reality.

The two pastors of the two largest churches in Montgomery County offered their facilities to host Samuel's funeral. We had two services because of the number of people who wanted to attend. Also, the first service was more for close friends and family. We met at Immanuel's Church on Thursday evening and at Covenant Life Church Friday morning. At each service, hundreds of people came at me from all directions. They were distraught and were concerned about our well-being. They were in shock too I suppose.

I did not want to be there. Masses of tear-stained faces pressed themselves into mine. Their bodies shook from sobs, and somehow I had to hold them up. I wasn't allowed to cry as any outbursts seemed to distress others even more. I had to be strong and believe for Sam's resurrection. The life seemed to drain out of me as I tried to console the mourners. *By God's grace, I can go through this*, I thought. Finally, everyone sat down, and the service began.

When they wheeled in Sam's casket that first night, I began to fall apart. Dan was up front, so I could not lean on him for comfort in that moment. A dear family friend, Don Finto, helped me pull myself together, and I began to focus on the goodness of the LORD and our ultimate victory over death.

The service included praise and worship. First was our own Messianic Jewish expression. It was crucial and it represented our roots. We included the "Kadosh, Kadosh" (Holy, Holy) song and the "Messianic Jewish Kaddish," a combination of the ancient prayer of praise to God said in the face of death. Additionally, we sang the songs of revival that had become part of the celebration of the church of the city and the revival hopes of our own day. Therefore, we sang songs like "Let it Rain" and "Shout to the LORD." Lastly, we sang the songs that had so positively affected Sam during our most recent visit to the Pensacola revival. These included "The Happy Song" and "Be Released."

The spirit of the LORD strengthened me during worship, and God turned my mourning into dancing. During the celebration of his homecoming, I actually was "released," as the song proclaims, to dance unto the LORD. I knew that God was able to raise Sam from the dead, but even if he didn't, he would see me through. Such worship produced a most unusual atmosphere of celebration in a service where the body of our young child lay lifeless.

Dan and I shared our hearts with those present. God means more to me than Samuel, and courageously I got up at the two services and proclaimed that death had been swallowed up by victory. I declared to the people that blessing upon blessing upon blessing would come to us as a result of this tragedy. Many stood up and praised God as the words were spoken. Satan would be sorry he struck Samuel; he had overplayed his hand again. What he meant for evil, God would turn for the good of those who believe.

Other dear friends spoke words of encouragement and built up our faith, though making sure that those who attended the service knew that our faith in God was not resting on the miracle of Sam's resurrection. They explained that we believed for a resurrection, but even if he did not come to life in this world, God had won the battle. Yeshua said with power, "I am the resurrection and the life. He who believes in me will live, even though he dies; and whoever lives and believes in me will never die. Do you believe this?" (John 11:25–26). If Samuel died, then his life would be like the seed that was sown into the soil so that there would be a great harvest. Mike Brown said that God would raise up one thousand Samuels to carry out his calling as a prophetic evangelist. The atmosphere was charged by the time the service ended.

After we took communion together, the time finally came for the leaders and intercessors to come forward and stand with us as we proclaimed life over Sam's body. How radical this was—I have never seen such an act of faith done at a funeral before. I was proud of my husband's courage to believe and to obey in the face of such agony and grief. Using a liturgy he wrote, we corporately declared resurrection life over Samuel. I have included Dan's actual liturgy that we used at both the Thursday night and Friday morning service. Because of Jewish tradition, we did not have Samuel's body embalmed, which made believing for a resurrection more feasible.

Resurrection Liturgy

(Spoken as an act of faith for any who have died before the fullness of years in the times of the restoration of the body of the Messiah, in anticipation of the general resurrection of the dead at the return of Yeshua the Messiah but also in the hope of the miracles of resurrection that are to occur in the last days, for such has already happened in many places in the world. Words of resurrection commands in italics to be read with fervor in raised voices.)

Leader: In John 11:24, Martha said to Yeshua of Lazarus her brother, "I know that he will rise again in the resurrection in the last day." This is indeed the hope of all who trust in Yeshua as Lord and Savior, for as the Scriptures say:

People: "Behold I tell you a mystery, we shall not all sleep, but we shall all be changed, in a moment, in the twinkling of an eye, at the last shofar blast: for the shofar will sound and the dead will be raised, imperishable and we shall all be changed."

Leader: However, even before that day there has been and will be resurrections from the dead to normal physical life. This is a sign from God and shows the resurrection to come. There are many credible testimonies in many nations of the resurrection of the dead. In the Bible we read such accounts. So Elijah the prophet healed a widow's son. He stretched himself upon the child three times and called to the LORD and said:

People: "Oh my God, I pray thee, let this child's life return to him." And the LORD heard the voice of Elijah and the life of the child returned to him and he revived, and Elijah said, "See, your son is alive."

Leader: Also, a dead man was resurrected when his body touched the bones of Elisha the prophet "and he stood upon his feet." Of Yeshua, we read the account of the son of the widow of Nain. "When he approached the city, a dead man was being carried out, the only son of his mother, and when he saw her, he had compassion on her, and he said, 'Do not weep,' and he touched the coffin and he said:

People: 'Young man, I say to you, arise.' And the dead man stood up and began to speak and Jesus gave him back to his mother. And great fear gripped them, and they glorified God."

Leader: And so with the daughter of Jairus, He took her by the hand and said:

People: "Child arise!" and she arose immediately.

Leader: Outside of his own resurrection, the greatest was that of Lazarus, for Yeshua said:

People: "I am the resurrection and the life, he who believes in me shall live even if he dies, and anyone who lives and believes in me shall never die."

Leader: After Lazarus was in the tomb for four days, and Yeshua said, "Did I not say to you, if you believe, you will see the glory of God?" and so they removed the stone... and he cried with a loud voice:

People: "Lazarus, come forth!" And he who died came forth, bound head and foot with wrappings, and his face was wrapped around with a cloth. Yeshua said to them, "Untie him and let him go."

Leader: Time does not permit to retell all of the accounts of Yeshua's own resurrection on the third day, or of Peter's raising Tabitha or Dorcas. Yeshua the Messiah gave the power to raise the dead to his body, the church, but in its broken and divided state, it has been rare in history. But he commanded:

People: "And as you go, preach saying, 'The kingdom of God is at hand, heal the sick, raise the dead, cleanse the lepers, cast out demons.'"

Leader: Yeshua prayed that his last days' congregation would be restored to unity, love, and power, and so it shall be; they will be one with the power to raise the dead.

People: "Truly, truly, I say to you, the works that I do... and greater works than these shall you do because I go to the Father. And whatever you ask in my name, I will do it that the Father will be glorified."

Leader: God is today restoring the church, the body of the Messiah. This is a time for a new liturgy, that in gatherings like this we call forth those who have died before the fullness of years—to believe and anticipate resurrection, and to give God opportunity to move in the name of Yeshua—for this is happening in our days!

(If the coffin is closed at the time, the leader may speak these words.)

Leader: Raise the lid of the casket.

Leader: We come as God's congregation, the body of the Messiah, representing the church in unity, rooted in Yeshua, and connected to Israel. We are one in his blood and in his bread and wine, the meaning of his broken body and shed blood. We have bound the powers of darkness by our union in his death and resurrection.

Shofar Leader: "Wake up, O sleeper, and rise from the dead." (At this time a shofar or multiple shofarim are blown with someone making proclamation from Ephesians 5:13. The one with immediate family authority would speak first— father, mother, or brother, guardian, spouse, elder, etc.)

Family Authority: "So as his (*father, mother, etc.*) I say, in the name of Yeshua, (*name of the person*), come forth, arise, and be resurrected from the dead."

Elders of the church of the city, Messianic Jewish congregations, visiting church leaders from other locales, and spouses who will exercise faith: "As elders of the church of the city, Messianic leaders, and supporters, we say, 'In the name of Yeshua, (*name of the person*), come forth, arise and be resurrected from the dead.'"

We even had four men holding long shofars, one standing at each corner of the open casket, blowing individually and then simultaneously to the four winds. We recited Ezekiel's account of the dry bones in chapter 37. Surely, there was enough faith to raise Samuel from the dead. But he did not move.

One time, a little child came forward and placed his hand on Sam's casket, speaking words of life over him. I began to have fearful thoughts. *Others must think we are out of our minds, that what we are doing is crazy! Certainly they will call the loony wagon to take us away to some insane asylum.* Yet, I wondered, what were more than forty mature, well-known leaders from across the nation and from Montgomery County doing standing with us? They couldn't all be crazy. Perhaps God was accomplishing something in a realm and time we could not comprehend.

Dan believed we were not calling forth Samuel alone, but he believed we were calling for the Samuel ministry to arise—even for the Samuels of the last days to come forth. Leaders of Messianic Jewish congregations and leaders of significant churches all gathered around the casket to stand together, believing with us.

Soon it was time again to be in that place to exercise faith for Samuel's resurrection. This time there was no communion service, but we rooted our unity in the service from the previous night's celebration. Once again, Dan explained what we were about to do. Don Finto stood by Dan as a support. We read the liturgy again. This time when we called for the leaders who would stand in faith for a resurrection of the dead, over forty pastoral leaders came forward.

We formed concentric, semicircles around the casket. First were the pastoral and five-fold leaders, then the intercessors, and lastly the people who would stand in faith with us. When the liturgy was read responsively with great fervor, the intensity increased. We gave ourselves time to allow faith to arise. Yet Samuel Peter did not literally resurrect.

The pallbearers came and took Sam's casket away after the Friday morning service and drove him to the gravesite. An upbeat praise song was sung, and we all filed out of the sanctuary. Did we fail? Was all this believing for nothing? Many have said that this was the most powerful funeral service they had ever attended and that their faith was not devastated but strengthened. They left that room in victory, not in defeat.

At the gravesite, the immediate family sat in chairs facing the earthen pit containing Sam's casket. After a brief ceremony and again speaking life over Samuel, people one by one began to throw shovels of dirt onto the casket. When it came time for me, I could not do it. I was angry and could not wait to get out of there. I thought, *Is this it, and is it over now, after six intense days of standing in faith? What now?*

We quickly moved to the limousine and drove off to the reception. That was when we were released to finally cry. I thought I would begin and it would never stop as days of accumulated stress and disappointment came crashing in on me. But I was only able to cry for a couple of seconds; the same happened to the others in the car. Right then, I put God in charge of my emotions and released my grieving process into his hands. I had been through grief work before and knew there was no escape. Either he would be the one in charge, or I would self-destruct from the pain. God proved faithful and never gave me more than I could bear.

The Gravest Gloom

What are those feeble Jews doing? Will they restore their wall? Will they offer sacrifices? Will they finish in a day? Can they bring the stones back to life from those heaps of rubble—burned as they are?

Nehemiah 4:2

The cords of death entangled me; the torrents of destruction overwhelmed me. The cords of the grave coiled around me; the snares of death confronted me. In my distress I called to the LORD; I cried to my God for help. From his temple he heard my voice; my cry came before him, into his ears.

Psalm 18:4–6

At home, after the funeral and the reception, we gathered some things together to take with us on our little getaway. We had been through such an intense week that we decided it was best for us to go where we could grieve alone. This went against the Jewish practice of sitting Shiva.[2] But perhaps that happened in the hospital and the days leading up to and including the funeral.

At first, I tried to do some bills, but found my hand-eye coordination was affected and I could not tell my hand what to do. It kept shaking, so I finally had a friend write the bills for me.

For a few days, I could not remember what occurred the week before Sam died, and I began to forget other important things. Sometimes I would be driving and forget where I was or where I was going. More and more, I began to forget people's names. I am still pretty bad at this, but I felt like a person who had had a stroke and couldn't get her body to do what her mind told it to do.

My ability to make decisions became impaired as well. Sometimes, in the grocery store, I would almost enter into a state of panic just trying to make simple product choices. For a while, being around crowds opened me up to feelings of panic. I could not relax as I kept expecting danger. When there was a sudden noise or some object fell to the floor, I would jump as if I were facing some life-threatening situation. All these responses, I learned, are typical of someone fighting Post Traumatic Stress Disorder (PTSD).

Along with this hypersensitivity to sudden noises, I would over-respond in an attempt to catch something as it was dropping. It felt like I was dealing with something life threatening or dangerous. Normal mishaps in life were magnified. This was because I had a stuck "feeler" and was operating in a mode of constant preparedness for action. Since trauma opens the door to unhealthy fear, it was easy for me to be startled or to go into panic.

I also experienced the trauma of memories from the day of the fire and the days of being in the hospital. I kept seeing Sam's body dragged from the fire and lying on the ground, unable to breathe. The look on his face haunted me for months because, even though it looked peaceful, there was no life. His body looked like an empty shell. Images of his grotesquely swollen body kept popping into my mind also. Others tried to reassure me that these images would fade and that I would once again remember the happy images of Sam's life. Thankfully, they were right, but I did not know it at the time.

Every few minutes, both during the day and when I woke up at night, the reminder of Sam's death would shoot through my body like an electrical shock. I could be involved in something else when suddenly the thought popped into my mind, Sam is dead, and my heart would be pierced as if I were hearing the news for the first time. It was worse at night because my sleep was fitful and my dreams seemed at times to be hallucinations. Yes, I did have nightmares of houses burning and of being trapped. These dreams would reawaken the fears of helplessness.

I dreamed of Samuel often; some were tormenting dreams, but most were healing in nature. A few times, when I was at my mother's house before she died, I experienced groaning, screaming, and deep, painful travail that broke through my dream world into my consciousness. I would wake up with tears running down my face. The prayers of many, I believe, sustained me and kept back the worst of the trauma. I know my experience could have been much worse. It is hard for those who have not gone through prolonged intense pain or grief to know how something could be experienced as both horrible and glorious when God reveals his grace.

After that, I entered a long season of restlessness. I would go from "room to room," "house to house," and "city to city" trying to find a place where my spirit could alight. My heart cried, "Where can I go to find peace?" When we went to the farm after the funeral,

I began to get restless after a couple of days and could not wait to go home. As soon as we got home and unpacked our bags, I wanted to leave again. I became restless and anxiously waited until I could change my surroundings. All summer long we went from place to place, but I was not able to be at rest. The world I had known and experienced for so long was no longer my home, but I was stuck in a place between two worlds; I could no longer be happy living here, yet it wasn't possible for me to live in my true home. I did not know how I was going to live in this tension.

Another factor that added to my trauma was living next door to the house where Samuel died. For six months, the burned furniture, toys, and rugs from the basement of the house remained piled high in the backyard. The outside walls of the house were charred and stained with black smoke. Windows were smashed and boarded up from the inside so the broken glass could still be seen. Every time we went in or out of our house, we were visibly reminded of the tragedy, and the sense of horror would often go through our bodies. Whenever it would rain, the smell of smoke from the burned house permeated the air of our house, and then not even the sanctity of our own home could protect us. But God did not give us more than we could bear, and his grace continued to sustain us in our weakness.

The hardest time came when, after eight months, they eventually began to repair the house. As they began gutting the inside of the house and dragging out all the devastation that had been hidden, I began to get more and more angry. This process somehow exposed the devastation still hidden inside of me, and I had to work through more pain.

Daily, we heard the pounding of hammers and the buzzing of saws. No longer was the inside of our house a safe place. Several of our friends began to strongly urge us to move, and, eventually, we reluctantly sought the LORD for confirmation. We had lived in this "dream house" for ten years, and we had so many happy memories there. Moving would create more stress, and that was the last thing I needed at the time, so I thought. But before long,

God tenderly convinced us it was time to move on, and he provided a beautiful townhouse for us to rent.

Within two weeks of putting our house up for sale, some perfect buyers made an offer, and we accepted. God, in his sovereignty, led a believing family to us who were overcoming a trauma themselves. The father had been in a building in Kenya that was bombed a year before. His life was miraculously spared, but several of their closest friends had died. When the mother came into our house, she immediately felt peace and knew it would be a place of healing for her. God had provided. They were eager to move in, and we were anxious to move out. What I thought would bring me great sorrow actually brought me great joy. On our moving day, I was never so happy to be leaving a place.

Also, during the first year after Sam's death, we had to release our two older children into courtship relationships, which soon turned into engagements. Right away we had to plan two weddings, which occurred within two months of each other. One wedding took place two months before our move and the other the day after we moved. Normally, moving in itself results in major stress, so how I was able to cope with two weddings and a move while still working through grief is just amazing to me. God's grace was working overtime, as this move was the easiest move ever for me.

I had made a lot of progress during that first year of grieving, and there were even some healthy signs emerging. However, there were other events that aggravated the wounds and even brought more injury. My mother died from pancreatic cancer six months after Sam died, and a close friend of ours died as well. Also, we were caught up in another battle over the life of a twelve-year-old boy in our congregation, who eventually died.

As if these were not enough, after pastoring for over twenty-two years, we turned our congregation over to a new pastor in June of 2000. We parted ways after a very difficult season of trying to make the transition of leadership work. So, on top of dealing with everything else, Dan and I were left without a home

congregation, and we experienced the pain of many broken relationships. The once thriving congregation dwindled to almost
forty attendees, and many of our precious friends scattered. We
felt cut off from the grace that is supplied through being knit
together with a local expression of a body of believers. Intense
loneliness was added to the trauma of these ongoing battles. And
as a result I lived in fear.

Wholeness is being able to walk in love, but where there is fear
it casts out love. Where fear dominates, there is separation and
division. Fear tormented me as I wrestled with guilt, with faith
issues, and with receiving the love of God. Perhaps these next few
chapters will provide a rare opportunity to see very closely what
that time was like for me.

During the years following this season of tragedy, I learned
to follow the leading of the Spirit as he comforted and guided
me. The truths I learned during this period have prepared me
for the work God has called me to do in these days before the
LORD returns. We are living in difficult times and the pressures of
life can cause even the strongest among us to faint from exhaus-
tion. Are our infrastructures strong enough to bear up under the
weight of confusion, terrorism, wars, and economic collapse? Will
Yeshua find faith on the earth when he returns? And, because of
the increase of wickedness (and hardship), the love of many will
grow cold. Will there be those who still love in the midst of mul-
titudes who hate?

In difficult times, the core of our being is tested and everything that can be shaken will be shaken. If Satan can weaken
the three pillars, faith (trust in God), hope, and love that hold us
up, then we will not be able to stand. I praise God for teaching
me and showing me how to strengthen my inner man, and for
empowering me by his grace to put these truths into action. It
is a miracle that I am still standing and that my heart remains
tender. My hope is strong, and my love has deepened. His faith
abides in me.

In pursuit of the treasures hidden in darkness I have found that not only is life itself a treasure but also I am a treasure. I was buried under layers of pain, guilt, and shame. I was a treasure hidden in darkness. Along the way God dug me out and cleaned me up. As I pressed into him he performed a miracle and is continuing this miracle. In his great mercy and love, his radiance transformed and is transforming this weak vessel. Oh, the poetic beauty of the treasure; Yeshua, being the great prize within this clay pot activating his special treasure: me!

Take heart, dear reader, for you are a precious and valuable treasure in God's sight and dearly loved. May God bring you out of any darkness you might be in and may the light of his glory and great love be revealed in your spirit. May you be blessed as you read and glean from the fruit of the field I have tilled, weeded, and watered over decades, but God provided the seed, planted it, and caused it to grow, yielding a crop a hundred-fold!

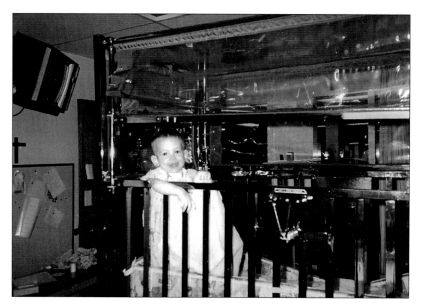

*Samuel recovering from a potentially fatal heart disease,
myocarditis, at age one*

Dr. Dan's favorite patient

My brother's car after his fatal accident

*Little did they know that they would be with
each other in heaven within a year*

Neighbor's House where Samuel slept the night of the fire

*The second story window from where the stepmother
jumped and ended up breaking her back*

The bookshelf where the candle was left to burn unattended

The ashes of the basement furniture where Samuel had slept

Samuel Peter Juster: Born March 29, 1986;
Went home to be with the Lord June 16, 1998

The grave marker In memorial of Samuel

PART TWO

Discovered Treasures

I will go before you and will level the mountains, I will break down gates of bronze and cut through bars of iron. I will give you the treasures of darkness, riches stored in secret places, so that you may know that I am the LORD, the God of Israel, who summons you by name.

Isaiah 45:2–3

Trust — The Answer

Is it not from the mouth of the most high that both calamities and good things come?

Lamentations 3:38

Then the LORD spoke to Job out of the storm: "Would you discredit my justice? Would you condemn me to justify yourself?"

Job 40:6, 8

When something bad happens, why do we insist on assigning blame to someone or something? I truly believe we want to place blame somewhere so as to somehow lessen the pain we're experiencing. For some reason, one of the first emotional issues a person goes through after experiencing a tragedy is coming to peace with the question of who was responsible. Guilty feelings seem to be one of the first areas we are hit with emotionally. Perhaps this is because we are trying desperately to go back in time, kind of like a "Back to the Future" scenario, in order to relive that moment the right way. *If only we had...* we think, as if we could have avoided the terrible loss.

In my case, my attempt to find fault was a way to somehow alleviate the first level of assault. There were only three ways I could go with my pain: I could go out, in, or up. The ball of blame kept getting passed in an attempt to find a focal point for relief. And so I passed the ball out toward others, blaming them at times; passing the ball back to myself, I blamed myself. I even threw the blame ball at God.

Oh the pain, the shock, the suffering, and the confusion I felt during the weeks following that tragic day! All the typically unanswered questions started to bombard me. *If only we had not let him go over there to sleep*, I thought. Why couldn't we have heard God's voice to take him home? Was there sin in our lives, a hardness of heart like King Saul, so that we could not hear? Did his death come as a result of lack of prayer covering from the outside? Did his death come because he spoke a curse of death over himself and I did not have him renounce it? Was it retaliation as a result of our prayer journey to Spain? Was it Satan or God or just our stupidity that caused Sam's death? So many questions were mine, but then I looked at all the circumstances surrounding his death.

The one answer I was looking for was much more complex than a simple cause and effect answer. In my search, I found these were the circumstances that led to Sam's death.

There was a storm that knocked out the electricity on Saturday around 4 p.m., and only our neighborhood remained without power into the night. There was no apparent reason why the electric company could not restore our power for fourteen hours. Then, there were the faulty smoke alarms that lacked battery backup. (How stupid to not have alarms that worked during a power outage, the most important time to have them working!) The landlords of the property next door had allegedly failed to get a building permit to finish the basement and, therefore, created illegal bedrooms. If they had obtained one, they would have had to pass inspection, which would have meant that they would have had to have different smoke alarms. Also, they would have been told not to have children sleep in the downstairs bedrooms—at least that was what came to our attention after the fire.

Shortly after the fire, a local newspaper printed an article commemorating the bravery of the firemen who rescued the boys and the courage of the boy who endured many surgeries and eventual leg amputations. In the article, they quoted the father as saying that the reason they left the candle burning was because Samuel was afraid of the dark. This pierced my soul as it appeared that the cause of the fire was Samuel. But, then, I had to work through this beam in my own eye, as I tried to place the blame on the parents for giving the children unsafe tapered candles. Additionally, I was disturbed that the parents had not checked to see if the children blew them out before bed. (There I went, passing the blame ball.)

Next, I reasoned that perhaps it was the teenager's fault because he decided to leave the candle burning, even if Sam did want the light afforded by the candle. (But I found out later that Samuel went to bed long before the teenager finally retired for the night.) I had begun to believe the typical lie that if I found out "who had done it," then I would feel better. Thankfully, this stage did not last long, and I did not hold bitterness in my heart toward the family or toward my own son.

Then I asked myself, "What chances were there that the candle would stay lit after falling many feet to the rug below? And what chances were there that the rug would catch on fire, since there was fire retardant in the rug? How about the fact that no one woke up until it was too late? Why did three boys live and the other two die?" On and on, I kept questioning.

After many weeks and months of going over these questions again and again in my mind, I finally made peace with God. The issues were not just issues of the heart but theological issues about what I believed concerning God's sovereignty and my free will. This first issue of causality went right to the heart of longstanding debate between Calvinism and Arminianism. It would have been so easy for me to believe in the Calvinistic view that God was in control and whatever happened was independent of any choices that I made. Because I was experiencing exaggerated fear and uncertainty, I wanted to no longer be responsible for my actions. But, alas, that is not what I believe the Bible teaches.

The other extreme, absolute Arminianism, which states that man is in control, frightened me too. If man were in control, we'd really be in trouble! Many times I have been wounded from proponents of this teaching. I could not accept a worldview that put man in an "if/then" bondage. If I obeyed, or if I confessed the promises enough, or fasted enough, or prayed enough, or spoke only truth-filled words, then nothing bad would happen.

According to this line of thinking, if something bad happened, it was because of what I did or did not do. Perhaps the cause of Sam's death came as a result of some wrong confession that came out of my mouth or because of my lack of faith or because of my not praying enough. (I can remember my mother blaming her son's death on the fact that she forgot to pray for him the morning of the accident.) I could, according to this view, determine my own destiny. This left the outcome of life subject to man's ability, and knowing my own limitations, my weaknesses of flesh, I sighed, "LORD help me."

Somehow, I was left with a paradox, and the truth stood somewhere between God's ultimate sovereignty and my absolute free will. I came to the conclusion that I would never find comfort in trying to figure out whose fault it was that Sam died. We all deserve to die, and we only live each day out of the abundance of God's grace and mercy. My comfort comes in the fact that in the Word it says that all the ways of the LORD are loving and faithful (Psalm 25:10).

As I continued to read Scripture, I could not get away from the numerous times it stated that God caused (or allowed) both good and bad things to happen to us. (Just look at the stories of Joseph, David, and Job). The way I began to see it was either God was LORD of all or he was not LORD at all. When we live long enough in this world, we face tragedy. More important than figuring out who was responsible for it are the choices we make after the tragedy has happened. I found I could get a lot of mileage out of suffering when I learned to yield to God in the midst of it. I discovered it not only drew me closer to him, but I began to learn just how truly trustworthy and loving he was and is.

We are admonished in Hebrews 12:7 to endure all hardship as discipline because God's discipline comes from a heart of love. He disciplines us for our own good, and what son does his father not discipline? The father loves the one whom he disciplines; otherwise, the child would be illegitimate. When God disciplines us, he is seeking to conform us into his likeness. We can see in the Word that discipline comes in many forms from the hand of God. Our nature that we are born with comes "broken" and needs fixing. It is painful when God tries to put us back together again. Sometimes, God uses circumstances to conform us, while at other times he may even use another's sin as his rod of correction in our lives.

Someone once confronted me with the questions of whether or not I thought suffering was God's perfect will for us. I would have to say, "No." However, this is not a perfect world. Like a doctor, God doesn't go around hurting people just because he loves to inflict pain. A doctor causes pain only as a means to bring health and healing to his patient. He is zealous for his patient to live and not die. How much more does God, who loves us with such a perfect love, want us to live and not die! Jesus came that we might have life and that we might have it more abundantly. And what doctor enters into our suffering as Jesus does?

Many believers, especially in the Western world, find it almost impossible to reconcile a loving God with suffering in his obedient children. In the minds of these believers, good people should not suffer; that is their idea of justice. We can see this attitude in the Bible too. In John 9:1–5, for example, the disciples and the Pharisees wanted to know who sinned—the blind man or his parents. Jesus's response was, "Neither… but this happened so that the work of God might be displayed in his life" (John 9:3). In yet another instance, some people told Jesus about the Galileans whose blood Pilate had mixed with their sacrifices. His response included a question about the sinfulness of the lives of those who died when the tower of Siloam fell. He said, "'Or those eighteen who died when the tower in Siloam fell on them—do you think they were more guilty than all the others living in Jerusalem? I tell you, no!'" (Luke 13:4–5). Even Peter must have had trouble with God's justice as he tried to dissuade Jesus from going to the cross.

In each of these instances, however, something must be understood, and this something is what I discovered in my own journey. When suffering through loss, through sickness, or through the effects of another's sin (apparent injustices), something holy is transpiring between the sufferer and God. It is crucial, therefore, that we do not give flippant answers. During these seasons we are being refined by God's holy fire.

Agabus warned the Apostle Paul about the impending danger and suffering awaiting him upon his arrival in Jerusalem. His friends pleaded with tears for Paul not to go, yet Paul strongly declared that he counted his life as worth nothing, "Why are you weeping and breaking my heart? I am ready not only to be bound but also to die in Jerusalem for the name of the LORD Jesus" (Acts 21:13). What if he heeded the warning and pleadings of his friends and did not obey God to avoid suffering? This life is not about our personal comfort but about the life of Jesus being preached and lived as a testimony—a triumphant testimony where his life is always swallowing up death.

What Dan and I went through these past years was holy and not to be evaluated in terms of "if/then." When we cried out to God for revelation concerning any specific sin we might have committed and he did not reveal any, then we knew that the suffering was necessary so that somehow the LORD would receive glory from our appropriate response to the suffering. This is a hard teaching but essential for what will be coming upon us in the last days. This position of embracing suffering—along with the position of embracing the promises of healing, protection, and provision—will always produce a sense of uncertainty in the person whose eyes are not stayed upon Jesus. Always, we are to choose life, but this stance does not contradict our position of yielding to God in the midst of our pain—of trusting him. This is victory!

In Deuteronomy 28–30, we are told about the consequences of choosing death or disobedience. The wages of sin is death no matter how we look at it. Death in all its various manifestations is ugly, repulsive, painful, and undesirable. God pleads with his people to choose life and, therefore, receive the blessings of life and not the curses of death. Nevertheless, there are consequences for our actions. When the principle of sowing and reaping kicks in, I do not know. Oh the grace and mercy of our God through the Messiah who loves us. The Word says that as far as the east is from the west is how far he has removed us from our sin. The psalmist says that God does not punish us according to what our sin deserves— yet there is the law of sowing and reaping. How all the more must we lean into God and obtain his grace and mercy to dwell in the midst of this mystery. We serve a God who appears to be paradoxical to the human mind, but God always acts in consistency with his character! He is always a God of love, full of goodness and mercy.

A father will often give a command to his child and give him the consequences for the breaking of that command. For example, a father may tell his child not to touch his stereo and warn him that if he does touch it, he will be disciplined. The child has a choice to obey or disobey. If he disobeys, the father then has several choices. Will he choose to carry out the discipline, or will he extend mercy? If he chooses to discipline the child, will he enforce a strict sentence or employ a lesser punishment? What kind of repentance should be required? What kind of comfort should be given? It seems that the father has more "control" than the child. The command and the consequences originated from the father; the child's only "control" was his choice to obey or disobey.

Was Sam's death preordained from the beginning of time? Is it, as it says in the Word, "all the days ordained for me were written in your book before one of them came to be" (Psalm 139:16)? Does God's foreknowledge mean everything is fixed ahead of time? I don't believe so; otherwise, there would be no sense to God's plea to choose life. There is a balance between the principle of sowing and reaping and the sovereign acts of God. God could have spared Sam's life supernaturally as he did the other three boys,' but he chose not to intervene.

I found that coming to the right theology or understanding of who caused these tragic events in my life did not and could not bring me the comfort and healing I needed. It came only as I learned to believe in the goodness of God and trust that his desire for me was that I prosper in this life. However, I had to work on other emotional issues too, like where I was going to get relief from all the pain and how to deal with the effects of prolonged depression and the waiting for relief. Also, I had to learn to live with being an emotional cripple for a long, long time and learn to accept my powerlessness. After all that, I had to face the emotional effect that my pain and suffering had on others and see how my family members would work through their own emotions. These were important stops along my journey of grief.

Accepting God's Will

Why are you downcast, O my soul? Why so disturbed within me? Put your hope in God, for I will yet praise him, my Savior and my God

Psalm 42:5

Depression is an enemy of our soul. It is a major manifestation of intense grief and hopelessness. It is one of the fruits of trauma. Depression saps one of energy and his/her will to live. When I fought depression, it felt as if I were wading through mud, and my capacity for activity diminished by fifty percent.

The emotional aspects of grief spilled over into the physical realm. For months, I did not feel like cooking or cleaning, and neither did I have the energy. Because I did not feel suicidal and rarely "felt" depressed, I did not think I was in depression. My doctor said I was in denial because I had all the symptoms of depression. I suffered from memory loss, had difficulty making choices, fought hopelessness from time to time, and often fought off panic. I experienced restlessness, fluctuation in my appetite, and impairment of my ability to exert myself mentally.

Because I had equated depression with "feeling" depressed, I found it difficult to believe the doctor's report. However, in the following months I came to "feel" depressed. After much reading and self-evaluation, I came to understand what depression meant, though *depression* is too broad of a term. So much of our abnormal behavior is categorized under the heading of depression. I discovered depression not only manifests itself emotionally but behaviorally and physically as well. I seemed to gain victory many times over my emotions, but over the other two areas I seemed powerless.

One time, however, when I came under an extended time of "feeling" depressed, God spoke to me so clearly: "*Patty, you expect to have a fellowship of my intimacy of joy and comfort, yet you refuse the fellowship of the intimacy of my suffering.* Your depression occurs because you are rebelling against the pain of grief, when this is my will for you at this time." First Peter 4:19 confirms what God spoke to me: "So then, those who suffer according to God's will should commit themselves to their faithful Creator and continue to do good." I needed to repent of my rejecting God's will for my life. Something broke in me as I wept and repented for my rebellion. Fellowship was then restored, and now, when I begin to "feel" depressed, I ask myself if there is some area of my life in which I am rebelling against God's will. When the area of resistance is uncovered and I repent, vitality returns. (Remember, not all depression is related to immediate results of rebellion; mine happened to be.)

Some aspects of my trauma, however, needed medication to help ease the stress. Spiritually, I found deliverance through embracing and yielding to God's will, but physically, I could not find relief until much later. I had panic attacks, insomnia, anxiety, and tremors. I became hypersensitive to sounds and outside stimuli (like objects falling or riding in a car close to a curb). I could not control these responses, which were part of the PTSD. Some people experience regular depression in this way, and it actually registers as a chemical imbalance. I also suffered from guilt that my faith wasn't sufficient to throw off the depression. Yes, there is a spiritual component to depression, but there also is a physical component. I needed a physical miracle in the same way a crippled person needs a miracle.

During the different seasons of going through the cycle of pain, comfort, and healing, I seemed to lose my will to fight. I would embrace life in the sense I was glad to be alive, but I just did not want to fight for my will to be expressed anymore. When Dan would ask me what I wanted to do, and even when he would give me a couple of choices, I would tell him I did not care. I felt that if I had no desires, then there would be nothing left for God to take away. If I had an agenda, then I would have to exert effort to see that it would get accomplished. With no goals or agendas, I could just flow with whatever happened. There was no frustration of unfilled goals or plans. It was the wrong kind of "deadness" that would sometimes masquerade as brokenness. In time, God showed me that if I lost my fight, I would die much in the same way as if my body stops fighting a physical ailment. If my body stops fighting off germs, I would die.

In my depression, I asked for prayer from many godly men and women, but after sharing my fears, they said they heard from God not to pray for deliverance for me. Go figure! Why was God refusing to deliver me from fear? These individuals sensed that God was going to give me release in another way. In the meantime, I had to resort to medication for a couple of months so that I would not flip out. The medication did not take away my emotional pain; it just calmed the other physical manifestations of grief so that I could concentrate on getting healed from the more serious dimensions of grieving.

I found accepting my suffering—accepting that it was according to God's will since I could not change what happened—enabled me to experience his grace. And his grace was sufficient for me, even when I felt like a basket case! Later, I was able to get off all medication. God does heal! More details of this process of receiving healing from trauma and grief can be found later in my book.

Waiting with Patient Endurance

I am still confident of this: I will see the goodness of the LORD in the land of the living. Wait for the LORD; be strong and take heart and wait for the LORD.

Psalm 27:13–14

Experiencing the pain of waiting was part of my trauma experience as well. I felt like I was caught in some kind of time warp. You might not think that waiting can be all that bad because there are different kinds of waiting. Waiting for Christmas, waiting for that chocolate cake to get out of the oven so you can let it cool enough to ice it and sink your teeth into it, waiting for your child to take his first step ... these occasions are what I call happy waiting. Then, there is the waiting that takes place in a grocery line, thus making you late to pick up your child at school and the person ahead of you has thirty-five coupons, food stamps, needs two items priced, and the cashier runs out of register tape right before she rings up your order. Also, there is the waiting in bumper-to-bumper traffic, or the waiting for your child to stop doing her fifty e-mails so you can do your one e-mail. These waiting occasions are aggravating and tension producing and stir up in us what should be resolved.

There is another type of waiting where there is nothing you can do but throw yourself into the arms of God. The waiting for that phone call from your doctor to get those test results, the waiting that takes place in the hospital waiting room while your child is in the intensive care unit and you do not know whether he is alive or dead, waiting for your mother to take her last breath so you won't have to spend another night watching her suffer, or the waiting for the pain to go away after the loss of a loved one. This type of waiting calls for patient endurance. Until you have experienced this waiting, you will not understand what endurance is. Through longsuffering, we learn to endure.

The hardest waiting of all for me is the waiting for the day when I may join the one I miss more than anyone else. After Sam died, I wondered how long it would be before I saw him. Would it be twenty years, thirty years, or maybe more? I am pressed daily into the arms of my savior, as he is my life. Slowly, I learned that waiting upon the LORD strengthened me and purified me of those reactions to lesser occasions of waiting. What used to bother me doesn't anymore. I have come to know God in ways I never knew. His grace is sufficient to get me through each day. Just when I feel that I am going under and can't take any more pain, God sends a message of grace—maybe some flowers, a note from a friend, or phone calls from individuals who just want to tell me they are praying for me. Before, I used to marvel at those who faced severe hardships and wondered how they got through them, but now I know. Outwardly, we are wasting away, but inwardly, we are being renewed day by day. Something is changing deep within. In the waiting, often we cannot "do" but must learn to "be."

Dan and I went through a long period of time before we heard from God about what our next stage of our ministry should be. Our accountability board decided we needed to go on a sabbatical for a year, so our waiting became even more pronounced. From January 1999 to January 2000, we were told to rest and only do things that brought us life. During this time, we sought the LORD and cried out to him for direction and for consolation. In a way, we did not want to move until we were sure his presence went with us. We so much wanted Sam's death not to be in vain, so we were waiting for marching orders that demonstrated some real purpose.

Since I was still suffering from heart insufficiency, I lacked energy. My doctor explained to me that it was like I had $100 to spend each day, and when it was gone, it was gone. And, if I pressed myself beyond that point, then I would be laid up for a couple of days recovering. Therefore, I spent a lot of time sitting in my recliner. Time seemed to drag as I sat and sat.

I found encouragement, though, through God's Word, specifically from the lives of his other servants who had long seasons of waiting. I thought of Abraham, Isaac, and Jacob, fathers in the faith. Through endurance and patience, they received those things promised them. And then, there was the story of the long time Joseph suffered in prison, waiting for the fulfillment of his dreams. It seemed that waiting was part of the training process of men and women of God.

I found that Scripture admonished us on several occasions to be patient. In fact, patience is one of the Fruits of the Spirit.

> Be patient, then, brothers, until the LORD's coming. See how the farmer waits for the land to yield its valuable crop and how patient he is for the autumn and spring rains. You too, be patient and stand firm, because the LORD's coming is near ... Brothers, as an example of patience in the face of suffering, take the prophets who spoke in the name of the LORD. As you know, we consider blessed those who have persevered. You have heard of Job's perseverance and have seen what the LORD finally brought about. The LORD is full of compassion and mercy.
>
> James 5:7–8, 10–11

Gradually, I began to hear God speaking to me about the importance of the lessons he was teaching me during this season.

June 1999

LORD, you have said in your word that through endurance and the encouragement of the Word we might have hope (Romans 15:4). You are the one who gives endurance and encouragement so that I might not fail (Romans 15:5). So how can I receive your gift of endurance? You have said in your Word that you will never grow weary or tired. You have promised to give of your strength and increase the power of the weak, of those who wait upon you and who put their hope in you. I will soar on wings like eagles, and will run and not grow weary. I will walk and not faint (Isaiah 40:28–31). LORD, give me grace to wait on you like the early disciples waited on you for the Holy Spirit before launching out on their mission. May I be like the wise virgins who were prepared for your delay by keeping an extra supply of oil with them. But LORD, I find this silence difficult. Why the silence? I feel like the psalmist, who said: "My soul faints with longing for your salvation, but I have put my hope in your word. My eyes fail, looking for your promise; I say, 'When will you comfort me?' Though I am like a wineskin in the smoke, I do not forget your decrees. How long must your servant wait? When will you punish my persecutors?" (Psalm 119:81–84).

God promised to give me his strength in my weak state as I waited upon him and put my hope in him. I found comfort in these words from Steve Fry:

> The LORD understands the emotional intensity of learning to believe even when we don't see. Have you ever considered that the LORD, when he sees us suffer, wants to rush to our side, even manifesting himself in physical form to comfort us? I assure you, in one sense he may long to ... but far more fundamentally, he doesn't, because that would only prolong our dependence on our senses, what we can see and touch—which would only addict us further to the temporal, material world. Ultimately, it would be the cruelest thing he could do, for we would not learn faith! Faith is the way we see in the spirit; it is the sensory organ of the spirit world.
>
> *A God Who Heals the Heart* by Steve Fry, 121

I had to learn to rejoice even when I did not see any fruit. I was not used to sitting still. I judged my worth by how much work I got done each day. When Dan would come home after work, he would jokingly ask me if I had been good. Then I would go through the long list of all the things I had accomplished that day. What a hard lesson for me to learn, being quiet before the LORD. I was concerned that God was going too far with this breaking process. But he showed me as long as I was capable of worship, my life was worthwhile! As long as I was willing to wait in his presence or just wait for him to meet my need, he was pleased.

> It is good to wait quietly for the salvation of the LORD. It is good for a man to bear the yoke while he is young. Let him sit alone in silence, for the LORD has laid it on him. Let him bury his face in the dust—there may yet be hope. Let him offer his cheek to one who would strike him, and let him be filled with disgrace. For men

are not cast off by the LORD forever. Though he brings grief, he will show compassion, so great is his unfailing love. For he does not willingly bring affliction or grief to the children of men. To crush underfoot all prisoners in the land, to deny a man his rights before the most high, to deprive a man of justice—would not the LORD see such things? Who can speak and have it happen if the LORD has not decreed it? Is it not from the mouth of the most high that both calamities and good things come?

Lamentations 3:26–39

In God's mercy, I slowly learned to be still and to seek to know him. I am the sheep of his pasture. He has created me. So, like Job, I put my hand over my mouth and waited for him. I stilled my spirit and quieted my soul; like a weaned child, my soul became quiet within me.

In due season, God revealed his plans for us, and they have been worth all the waiting! In January 2000, Dan and I began to travel full time. We went all over the country, strengthening the fifteen to twenty Tikkun congregations for which we were then responsible.

Though going through the "death" experience with our home congregation, Beth Messiah, was painful, how thankful Dan and I are to know that the congregation is still alive! Out of the labor of her members, she has birthed perhaps over fifty workers into the mission field, birthed Tikkun, and was one of the main Messianic Jewish congregations that birthed the Union of Messianic Jewish Congregations, an organization that ties together over ninety congregations worldwide that is more of a unity blend organization. So her fruit remains. Even though she is cut off from both her fathers and her future enjoyment of her "grandchildren" at present, we are trusting God for her complete restoration.

We have on the Tikkun American and International Board friends who have remained faithful for almost thirty years! They have been such a support and an encouragement. We have walked through so much together, and it is such a joy to work with them.

Also, Dan and I go to various churches and share with them about their Jewish roots and raise support for our new ministry in Israel. Dan and I, along with our youngest daughter, Simcha, received our citizenship in Israel in the summer of 2000. So, as part of our travels, we are seeking those whom God has chosen to be the champions of this work. We are so excited about this new direction in our lives. It seems like I was being prepared for this season in my life for years. Dan and I had to be able to identify with the suffering of the people we were going to serve.

We are based just outside of Jerusalem, and are working in a discipleship training school for Hebrew-speaking young people. We are especially interested in the young soldiers coming out of the army. Our daughter, Simcha, actually served in the army for two years. We are living in Israel six months or more out of the year. I also am interested in supporting a healing center for drug addicts, unwed mothers, the sick, weary leaders, and those who are traumatized. I would like to see this center provide grief counseling and personal care. It is a big vision, but I have already met several people whom God has laid this desire upon their hearts.

I think God knew we needed the time of rest, as now we are on the go all the time. In fact, we fly almost one hundred thousand miles each year now! We are rarely in the same congregation two weeks in the row! So if you are in a season of waiting, just wait, enjoy the time of rest and patiently endure. It probably just means you will be very busy in the days ahead.

In the next chapter we will pick up my grief journey again as I did not arrive at this place of victory overnight. It has been a long hard road to recovery, and I invite you to continue walking with me as I reveal to you many of the hidden treasures I found along the way that were refined in the fires of mystery.

Getting Comfortable
with Comfort

When I was in distress, I sought the LORD; at night I stretched
out untiring hands and my soul refused to be comforted.

Psalm 77:2

Since I was experiencing so much pain, there were periods of restlessness. How like the time when I was in physical pain resulting from my back surgery—I wanted relief! No one could take away the pain completely, except through narcotics, but others could make me comfortable so I could better endure the pain. I think it is important to understand the limits of trying to give and receive comfort. If I had wrong expectations from myself or others, it could set me up for more pain.

When I was in the hospital, nurses came into my room to straighten my bed sheets, fluff my pillow, bring me fresh water, or rub my back. They accepted the limits of their ability to relieve pain, but they were competent in making me comfortable so I could better endure the pain. In dealing with my loss of Samuel, I was in search of comfort, yet I often resisted the comfort of others.

Dan and I received so many cards. The ones that meant the most to us were the ones that talked about the memories a person had about Samuel and how much he or she appreciated him. I grew to dislike cards that had no personal note, just a signature. Though I am sure the senders of such notes were simply trying to let us know they cared, I found them to be so comfortless at the time.

Cards and flowers were lifelines in those early days. However, I used to get sad when I received flowers that perished; I wanted living plants that would be there in a week, a month, or a year. Every time I received a plant, I would remark how glad I was that I had something that wouldn't die in a couple of days. The last thing I needed was a reminder that life was but a vapor!

But one time, God especially ministered to me through a precious gift of a floral bouquet from my sister-in-law. I received it around the time of Samuel's and my birthday. It was a season of depression, and I was questioning the wisdom of God in giving us Samuel if he knew how much pain his loss would bring. As I gazed at the intrinsic beauty of the individual flowers, I heard the voice of the LORD tenderly speak to me. He asked me, "Would you rather I had not made these flowers? You know that they will perish in a few days, and yet you are not letting that fact diminish your enjoyment of them." I saw that I had to look at my relationships the same way and accept them as gifts that are temporary in this life. I returned to an old truth of learning to love to the fullest, not holding back in fear, even if the relationship was only to be for a few short years. That limited time of enjoyment in my relationship with Samuel was worth it, as it will be with me for eternity.

When the "excitement" of phone calls, flowers, cards, and visitors subsided, I thought, *What now?* All the activity had distracted me, but now I could no longer avoid facing the real issues confronting me like, *What am I going to do with all the pain of grief that is seeking to undo me? How do I bear up under it? Is there no balm in Gilead? Where can I go to find solace and comfort to ease the pain, or is my wound incurable? Will I be able to receive comfort, or will I be, like Rachel, weeping for her children?*

Many tried to comfort me, but often they stumbled over their words and ended up doing more harm than good. And then, even if another were comforting "righteously," often I would still refuse to be comforted. I did not want others to take away my pain. Pain was all I had left of Samuel, a vivid reminder that he lived and was connected to me. However, no amount of effort could bring Sammy back. How similar I was to others in the Bible. There was Jacob, who, according to Genesis 37:34–35, refused to be comforted upon hearing Joseph had been killed by some beasts. And then there was Asaph, who sought the LORD in Psalm 77, and yet he too refused to be comforted. Lastly, there was the prophetic reference to Rachel in Jeremiah 31:15: "This is what the LORD says: 'A voice is heard in Ramah, mourning and great weeping, Rachel weeping for her children and refusing to be comforted, because her children are no more.'" Although I was among good company, I had to relinquish my refusal and begin to learn how to receive comfort, just as I had learned physically to allow the nurses to help make me comfortable. In other words, I learned to receive comfort as others tried to make me comfortable with their expressions of comfort.

I came to understand that the grief journey was a gift from God and should not be moved through hastily. I did not want a quick fix, yet I wanted everything to be all right. I guess I really did not know what I wanted. I knew that grieving was a process a bereaved person must go through (unless God supernaturally removes the grief). Grief was not something to be feared. I wanted others to know and understand and to be at peace in my presence—to let me hurt!

I came to dread questions like "How do you feel?" or "How are you doing?" These provoked me at times to question internally, *How do they expect me to feel? Do they really want to know, or are they asking these questions out of habit? Should I put on a front because, after all, I do not want to appear as a less-than-victorious believer?* I wondered if my friends could really handle the depths of my pain, thinking they, perhaps, might become frustrated or discouraged by my very presence. Such questions really could not be avoided, and I found them to be part of the liturgy that was expressed to the bereaved.

I appreciated those who called and said they were thinking of me and had been praying for me regularly. Often, they would ask if there was anything specific for which they could pray. People's prayers were like precious gold to me. Others would call and ask me how my grief work was coming along, or they would ask me unrelated questions. My life was more than just the experience of grieving. However, I did love to talk about Samuel and how God was going to bring good out of his death.

Another comfort came from human touch. When I was going through the worst times in the hospital with Samuel, I kept one woman friend on each side of me, and they held me tight. They did not say much, but they comforted me by their presence. It was like they were adding their strength to mine. These women would then try to get the men to cuddle Dan; I guess that is going too far for men! For this reason, I believe, it put more stress on me. I could receive hugging comfort from other women easier than Dan could from men. That left most of the physical comfort up to me.

I used to think that hugging was about the only real comfort another human being could give a bereaved person until I became a recipient of extravagant love on several different occasions. We were blessed to have many friends come to our side and lavish this kind of love on us through preparing meals, cleaning the house, doing errands, taking care of phone calls, writing thank you notes, taking us out for dinner, or letting us stay in their house. I do not know if Dan and I could have survived without the abundant love coming from those who cherished us.

Sometimes, I found comfort in the strangest things, such as hearing from others who had it worse than me. Shortly after Samuel's death, I received letters from parents who had lost children. One family in New York had lost all their three children in a car accident. From Texas, I heard from a parent who lost four of her five children in a car accident, and from Virginia, I heard from a pastor who lost all four of his children to a genetic disease. Upon contacting them, we received strength and hope as they testified to the grace of God in the midst of their pain. Somehow, they made it through and encouraged us that we would too.

Other emotions besides grief accompanied my pain. Sometimes I experienced anger, not necessarily anger against God, but anger because of the apparent injustice of the loss. The mixture of anger with grief was perhaps the greatest hindrance for my receiving comfort. I felt a sense of injustice. *Why did I have to be chosen for this tragedy? It just isn't fair! Others more unrighteous than I never lose their children.* In my agonized reasoning process, I appealed to the fact that I had served God faithfully all these years, and yet this was what I received back for my faithfulness. *If that was how God treated the one whom he loved, then how would he treat the one he hated? I thought.*

I came to believe that anger was normal and not something to be feared. It was natural to get angry when tragedy struck. I read the stories of many great men and women of faith who had become angry with God during some part of their journey. The pages of the Bible are filled with such stories. I saw that God could handle my momentary outbursts of anger. I found it to be much healthier to express it than to deny my anger or to suppress it. Besides, God was my friend, and our relationship could withstand a little friction. Anger only became a problem if I misdirected or prolonged it. I could not allow myself the luxury of indulging in long seasons of upset, as anger is a very intense emotion and can become destructive. My anger diminished as I came to understand that God was sovereign and that he was indeed acting with my best interest in mind. Again, it came down to learning to trust in the goodness of God.

But, even with a contrite and believing heart, it was often very difficult to receive comfort because the pain was so great. Another hindrance to receiving true comfort, I found, was expecting too much from people or expecting to heal quickly. It took a long time to heal; in fact, I'm still healing. I just couldn't expect the pain to suddenly disappear. The comfort I received in the beginning, at most, gave me strength and hope that one day I would get through. I was made "comfortable." Often, even though I was receiving comfort, I did not feel a lessening of pain when others tried to console me and be friendly. Sometimes, this triggered anger toward the person who was trying to comfort me. Others could sense when I was expecting them to do what only God could do, and they would try to avoid me, seeing me as the "needy" person. It even would tap into the consoler's own sense of inadequacy. I had to remember that God was my comforter, and though he used others, no one else or anything else would ultimately be able to satisfy the pain of my emptiness.

It did not take long to discover what kind of activities brought us comfort and what did not. In the early stages of grief, Dan's and my field of "allowable" activity was much narrower than it was later on. In the beginning, we couldn't watch movies or get involved with other passive entertainment. If we did, in our distracted state the grief would come crashing in upon us, and it became almost unbearable. I think the reason for this was that we had to be actively involved in fighting off the spirit of death, the crushing weight of grief that did not give us a break. *We could not let grief work back up. Grief work was an active pursuit.*

Also, we found that we had to avoid large crowds and party atmospheres. Being around large groups of people put stress on us to converse. It took a certain energy level to maintain good conversations with people we did not know. I had always experienced a certain level of insecurity when I was in a large group of people, and grief only accentuated this sense. Many times, I felt people staring at me, and I felt their pity. That was most uncomfortable. Unsolicited pity was most grievous to us. It just seemed like wherever I went I had this neon sign blinking inside of me announcing that I was an emotional misfit, a cripple. A party atmosphere just magnified the different world of pain and loneliness I was in. The contrast of worlds was too great at this season in my life.

We learned from these experiences how to spend our time more wisely. How easily we were deceived into thinking certain things would bring comfort when actually they produced greater emptiness. Entertainment, working harder, or "checking out" did not bring the comfort we were looking for. We had to remember that we were particularly vulnerable at this time and couldn't afford to do anything that would open us up to greater attack. We knew that distractions would not bring true comfort and healing. We knew they would only intensify the problem although they appeared to dull the pain for a while. Only God was the one who could take away the pain, yet we could not avoid walking through the dynamics of receiving his comfort through the expressions of others.

Receiving the God of All Comfort

Praise be to the God and Father of our LORD Jesus Christ, the father of compassion and the God of all comfort, who comforts us in all our troubles, so that we can comfort those in any trouble with the comfort we ourselves have received from God. For just as the sufferings of Christ flow over into our lives, so also through Christ our comfort overflows.

2 Corinthians 1:3–5

Psalm 23:4 speaks of the comfort we should receive from the Shepherd's rod and staff. God's discipline shapes and directs our life toward his divine purpose for us, our holiness. When a child is free to do what he wants without the benefit of boundaries and consequences, then he becomes anxious and unhappy. God has created us to be like him and to be partakers of his holiness. We are happiest when we are being and behaving like him. We must remember that Hebrews 12 follows the great chapter recounting the awesome faith of our forefathers who endured hardship and suffering for the sake of the promises of God. Even Yeshua endured great suffering for the fulfillment of these promises. In reflecting on these verses about God's divine discipline in our lives I had to rise above a human understanding of this term discipline. Did I view God as punishing us for some sin we have committed? Though God's discipline of us has some analogous relationship to our human father's discipline, God's dealing with us goes beyond this analogy. When the reasons for our suffering and hardship are shrouded in mystery, we are thrown into a position of ruthless trust. It is a refiner's fire. *I don't know why I am suffering, but I entrust my spirit into the hands of God as he is able to use whatever comes my way for my benefit, my righteousness, and future glory.*

Ultimately, grieving is a process of becoming reconciled with God. It becomes a time of reconciling the devastation of loss with a loving and good God. It is a time of dealing with the apparent injustice. When a father disciplines his child for wrongdoing and the child feels that his treatment is unjust, the child will close up and harden his heart. He will not receive healing when the father tries to comfort him. The child is only comforted when he is in agreement with the father that he deserved the discipline. No comfort can take place when a person is in rebellion to the circumstance in which he finds himself. We need to count all hardship as discipline and must yield to the father of our spirits and live. In our contriteness, we will then reap a harvest of peace and righteousness.

It is difficult to accept discipline from God sometimes, as we think he is like our human parents, who may have disciplined us in anger or disciplined us wrongly. We must not project our human father onto our heavenly father. God's discipline is always for our good, not because we necessarily did something wrong, but because he is working to conform us into his image. I have found very little of his discipline in my life has to do with punishment of something I did wrong.

God loves us and has our best interest in mind. Can we grasp this truth? Trusting and submitting to God in the midst of suffering are keys to gaining comfort. *When I had come to peace with God's ways, then I was able to receive his comfort.* That was not an easy task. If I did not push through to an understanding of God's goodness in the midst of the loss, then I would have hardened my heart and stayed in my pain. I bring up the example of the Israelites here because understanding God's dealings with them has helped me in coming to terms with God's discipline in my life. I feel like God has brought me through so much in order that I can someday minister to the pain in the heart of the Jew. I long for the day when the Jewish people will come to the revelation of the goodness of God in their lives. It has been their struggle throughout their history.

The Israelites did not have eyes to understand the discipline of the LORD and ended up hardening their hearts against Moses and God. How many of us are being tripped up because of our lack of understanding God's discipline in our lives and equating his discipline with his apparent lack of love or goodness? We read of how their lack of understanding God's love led them to rebel against his commandments.

But you were unwilling to go up; you rebelled against the command of the LORD your God. You grumbled in your tents and said, "The LORD hates us; so he brought us out of Egypt to deliver us into the hands of the Amorites to destroy us."

Deuteronomy 1:26–27

Remember how the LORD your God led you all the way in the desert these forty years; to humble you and to test you in order to know what was in your heart, whether or not you would keep his commands. He humbled you, causing you to hunger and then feeding you with manna, which neither you nor your fathers had known, to teach you that man does not live on bread alone but on every word that comes from the mouth of the LORD. Your clothes did not wear out and your feet did not swell during these forty years. Know then in your heart that as a man disciplines his son, so the LORD your God disciplines you.

Deuteronomy 8:2–5

Moses summoned all the Israelites and said to them: your eyes have seen all that the LORD did in Egypt to Pharaoh, to all his officials and to all his land. With your own eyes you saw those great trials, those miraculous signs and great wonders. But to this day the LORD has not given you a mind that understands or eyes that see or ears that hear.

Deuteronomy 29:2–4

You see, the Israelites did not understand that God was trying to break them of their self-sufficiency and stubbornness so that they would do his will rather than their own will. God's desire for them was that they might prosper in the land he was giving them. They misinterpreted their painful experiences as being God's desire to kill them. But God wanted to bless them; how far they were from the truth! Rather than trust God in the midst of their trials, the Israelites grumbled and complained and then threatened to kill Moses and go back to Egypt. In Isaiah 6, it states that the Israelites are under a curse because of their unbelief. They are plagued with calloused hearts for a season until the fullness of the Gentiles comes in. Then, they will come to the point of revelation that God is really for them and not against them. They will come to their senses, much in the same way as the prodigal in the story of the son who went astray. They will come to a place where they will turn toward Jesus and be healed.

The story of King Nebuchadnezzar in the book of Daniel illustrates this point of how a person can come to a moment of enlightenment. Here was a king who became proud. God removed him from his kingdom for a season. When he came to his senses, he understood that God was sovereign and that he could do anything he wanted. Nebuchadnezzar broke forth into praise when he came to the point of revelation; he came to understand and believe in the goodness of God.

> Immediately what had been said about Nebuchadnezzar was fulfilled. He was driven away from people and ate grass like cattle. His body was drenched with the dew of heaven until his hair grew like the feathers of an eagle and his nails like the claws of a bird. At the end of that time, I, Nebuchadnezzar, raised my eyes toward heaven, and my sanity was restored. Then I praised the Most High; I honored and glorified him who lives forever. His dominion is an eternal dominion; his kingdom endures from generation to generation. All the peoples of the earth are regarded as nothing. He does as he pleases with the powers of heaven and the peoples of the earth. No one can hold back his hand or say to him: "What have you done?" At the same time that my sanity was restored, my honor and splendor were returned to me for the glory of my kingdom. My advisers and nobles sought me out, and I was restored to my throne and became even greater than before. Now I, Nebuchadnezzar, praise and exalt and glorify the king of heaven, because everything he does is right and all his ways are just. And those who walk in pride he is able to humble."
>
> Daniel 4:33–37

There came a point in my suffering when, through the revelation of the Holy Spirit, I could say, "Just and true are your ways, oh LORD!" You could say I came to my senses. I came to trust a loving and good God who truly was out for my good. To get to this point was long and hard, but oh, the victory that is the LORD's and ours when we can see this truth. We can sing with the saints of old who have overcome:

> Great and marvelous are your deeds, Lord God Almighty. Just and true are your ways, king of the ages. Who will not fear you, O Lord, and bring glory to your name? For you alone are holy. All nations will come and worship before you, for your righteous acts have been revealed.
>
> Revelation 15:3–4

Jesus said that it was necessary for him to go away so that he could send the comforter. The role of the Holy Spirit to bring comfort to me grew over the years. In the midst of intense loneliness, when I felt like there was no one who could share the pain with me, I had the awesome sense of gratitude to God for giving me this gift. He said he would not leave us as orphans! Through his Spirit, he never leaves me nor forsakes me. He always knows what I think and feel and is right there with me. So many times I wished that I could get inside Dan, into his emotions and thought processes, and I desired that he would be able to know me in that intimate way too.

One time I visited my then three-year-old granddaughter, Layel, and she was so thrilled to see me she could not stop saying how much she loved me. In response I told her that I loved her so much that I could eat her up. Shocked, she responded, "Nana, we don't eat people. We eat food." Of course, I then had to explain what I meant. I was expressing in human language my desire for her to be on the inside of me and me on the inside of her. Alas, only the indwelling presence of the Holy Spirit, as comforter, can express this kind of intimacy. That is why the Holy Spirit became so precious to me. Here was one who lived on the inside of me and expressed the emotions of God the Father to me. It was a mystery how the Father, Son, and the Holy Spirit all worked together to bring comfort and healing. Even though their working in my life cannot necessarily be separated into their individual personalities,

I wanted to make sure I gave recognition to each member of the godhead in this process of restoration.

Part of our encouragement comes from understanding that when we are comforted by God, and even healed, we can be used by him to comfort others. I loved this teaching that I heard given by Dottie Schmitt, a dear pastoral friend of mine. Some have even been called upon to comfort Jesus himself. She talked about the life of Mary, the sister of Lazarus. She said that at first, Mary learned to linger at Jesus's feet, listening to him and worshipping. This prepared her for when she would languish at his feet at the death of her brother. And this suffering deepened her so one day she could lavish love on Jesus's feet by pouring expensive oil over them and wiping them with her hair. Her extravagant love flowed from a heart broken by sorrow, and out of that brokenness, she comforted Jesus. Through my pain, I have come to understand that Jesus still needs the Mary ministry to lavish love on him. Our worship and obedience still comfort him in his suffering over the loss and the pain of others. It is the balm of Gilead. May I become like Mary to his heart!

As someone who has worked through a lot of grief in her life, I have found there is no comfort like the comfort I get from the source of all comfort, God. My favorite place to grieve was in the middle of a worship service where the Spirit of the LORD was powerfully present. In that kind of atmosphere, I could release the tears of grief in a place of safety and receive immediate comfort from the Comforter. Sometimes, the pain would be so great that, in the midst of praise and worship, I would be deeply sobbing and crying out, "I hurt, I hurt—but I worship you—I love you." Truly, those times were glorious as God would reach down and draw me up into heavenly places. As much as I hated the pain of grieving, I asked God in my better moments not to take away the pain until he worked his glory in me. I wanted to gain full benefit from this suffering since there was no escape. I sensed God's greater purpose for me in the midst of the pain, and he imparted faith in me that I would gain greater intimacy and blessing if I continued to yield my spirit into his hands. "Holy, holy, holy, is the LORD God Almighty." He is worthy of all our praise!

Grief's Competition

[Job's] wife said to him, "Are you still holding on to your integrity? Curse God and die!" He replied, "You are talking like a foolish woman. Shall we accept good from God, and not trouble?"

Job 2:9–10

Like Job and his wife, Dan and I suffered from a grief that found us at times on opposing sides. By the grace of God, I did not give my husband the same council that Job's wife gave him, but losing our child put a tremendous stress on our marriage. We both were reeling from the pain of loss and were powerless to help comfort each other in the early stages of grief. We were told that many couples who lose children end up divorced. I now understand why.

Our marriage relationship became threatened to the point where I was wondering if we would become part of the statistics of those who did not make it. I kept misinterpreting my husband to be competing in his pain with my pain. Grief is like that. It appears to be in competition with itself. It seemed like whenever I brought up how bad I felt, Dan would tell me how much worse he felt. I tried to gain comfort through sharing my heart only to be met with how bad off he was, and he tried to do the same only to be met with how truly bad off I was. Can you imagine going to a counselor to talk about your marriage, and you only get into your story for five minutes when the counselor starts to talk about how bad his marriage was—for the rest of the hour? That's what it was like trying to talk to each other. Instead of being able to give and receive comfort and counsel, we both simply vented our feelings without embracing or comforting each other. My grief was in competition with his grief, or so it seemed.

Sometimes, Dan would misinterpret my silence and make statements that I was doing better than he was. Just because I sometimes broke through the pain when I received revelation about some aspect of God's character did not mean I still didn't hurt. I wrestled with thoughts like, "Do I not talk and just let my husband talk, but, if I do, will he think my silence as an indication that I do not hurt?" I would just be frozen in my inability to respond. If the truth were known, he was actually the saintly one during this time. After the first couple of months, he calmed down, and I became the testy one.

I became easily bothered by his moods. For example, when we were in times of worship, I would churn inside because he rarely opened his mouth. This went on for several months. One time, he did not even come to hear a special speaker, and I made apologies to this man. He gently admonished me to give my husband some space and said that he did not need any excuse.

Also, it seemed like Dan was always retelling the story of the weeks surrounding Samuel's death. Every new person became a recipient of another recounting of what happened. I felt like I was never able to tell my story (which wasn't true) and experienced a sensation of suffocating under his grief. There seemed to be no room for my pain.

In addition to this problem, I could not handle Dan's pain along with my pain. He expected comfort from me, and I could not give him any. Because I loved him, I couldn't bear to see him in pain and often did not want to be in the same room with him because of it.

My intimate life with Dan was also affected. Often my energy level was depleted, and I felt like I could not give of myself in any way to another. Through time, that changed. The good news was that Dan and I achieved a greater level of intimacy because of what we went through together. We became each other's hero. Hugging in the midst of our brokenness had become like "super sex," probably because most of our protective walls were down. Today, we are in awe at the level of liberty we feel toward each other. I feel like I have fallen even more in love with this man and cherish his friendship.

Then, there was the problem of misplaced anger. Often, Dan and I would take out our frustration on each other, the children, or the dog when our real problem was that we were just hurting over our loss of Samuel. It was helpful at these times to hug the other person and say, "You are really hurting now, aren't you?" We had to cut each other a lot of slack.

Please understand, what we went through was normal. It was just that we both were screaming out for relief and could not find it. We had to be patient and remind ourselves that others got through the grieving process and so would we. We just made a commitment to work things through no matter how much it hurt. Since we had a good marriage going into this tragedy, by God's grace we were able to weather this storm. At different stages along the way, we did go to others for help, and they provided a context of support and encouragement for us. Plus, we knew that God had a purpose for our lives and that we could not give up. We knew we had to fight this battle of embracing life again together.

Working my grief through in the midst of others who were grieving demanded a lot of patience, a lot of grace from God. I would try to go to different members of my family for comfort only to run into their wall of pain. Here my grief went again, competing with the grief of others. I felt that I could not freely bare my heart; it was as if my words fell to the ground.

Dealing with the grief of our children presented an even bigger problem. Each one handled it differently. Dan and I tried very hard to keep the communication lines open so that we all could discuss our pain freely. Unfortunately, I think the children often experienced the same frustration Dan and I had when we tried to comfort each other. They kept running into our wall of pain. The children so much wanted our family to return to normal that they tried desperately to say the right things to take away our pain. Our older children sometimes expressed that they did not even want to hang out at home anymore because they couldn't bear to see us in so much pain. We reassured them that what we were going through was normal and that one day we would come through it. We spoke out of faith and not feeling that one day joy would be restored. Just because we were hurting over our loss of Samuel did not mean that we did not love them. Life had to go on. The children had to go to school, work, and maintain relationships. We all learned that the world does not stop moving just because someone dies. Others looking from the outside into our daily life probably would not notice that much had changed. What could not be seen was the internal makeover that was taking place in each of our lives.

However, as the years past, it became more and more evident that our children suffered in ways we were not aware. Our own pain blocked us from seeing their need for outside counseling. Our older two children, Ben and Becca, had some relief in their suffering as they were in courtship relationships during their intense season of grief. They found comfort in their newfound love as their future spouses took on the role becoming the listener. For them life pretty much went on as usual as they had a hope and a future! Their latent trauma became more evident, however, when they began to have children and unresolved fear of death began to surface.

Ben's presence the first few months after Samuel died was a tremendous blessing. He had a strong friendship with Samuel, and Sam's death left quite a hole in Ben's heart. When Ben was in Ethiopia at the time of the fire, he was fighting with the rest of the mission team for the life of Samuel. When he received news of Samuel's death, he and Becca made the difficult choice to stay in Ethiopia instead of coming home for the funeral. They believed that God would honor their faith by raising Samuel from the dead. When this did not happen, Ben shut down and withdrew into himself. He went into an almost catatonic state, and no one could get him to talk. Finally, as others surrounded him and prayed for him, he came through and talked. Later, he told people that he was raging inside and did not want to speak for fear that he would curse God. But, praise God, he came through this fire and has remained faithful to God. When Ben came home from Ethiopia, he put off getting a job so he could be a comfort to Dan and me by just being with us. Our friendship has deepened, and our warm regards and respect for one another has increased. Ben gets great joy out of playing the keyboard and guitar for worship on occasion. All those years of music lessons have paid off!

Ben married a wonderful, godly woman, Lorena. After many years of working in the human resource field in various companies, Ben is finally coming alongside his dad as director of operations of Tikkun Ministries. We are privileged to have them live a mile from us in Boca Raton, Florida. They are always practicing hospitality and are especially a blessing to us when we are in Israel, taking care of our stateside affairs.

Lorena has become like a daughter to me, and we regularly get to together for discipleship and friendship over dinner. I love it when she calls me several times a week. When we were in the hospital sitting vigil over Samuel for forty-eight hours, Lorena was right there with us, upholding us with hugs and prayers.

These precious children have given us three wonderful grand-children, Abigail, age nine; Nathaniel, age seven; and Andrew, age three. Truly, they are a delight and bring us much joy. I love the way Abby runs into my arms calling, "Nanna, Nanna," and then smothers me with kisses and hugs. She tells me again and again, "Nanna, I love you!" She is so abandoned in her love for others. And Nathaniel has grown into such a sensitive young man and loves to play "monster" with his grandfather. Abby and Nathan play for hours by themselves and rarely seem to have the sibling rivalry that so many children experience. And their youngest, Andrew, can capture even the hardest of hearts with his whimsi- cal smile. Just hugging him releases such peace and comfort to the hurting soul.

Rebecca finished up her nursing degree during the two years following Samuel's death. She had experienced a lot of stress over the loss of Samuel. Instead of taking time off to grieve, she went right back to work to earn money for college and then back into her nursing program at the end of the summer. I wish I had had enough sense to keep her home for the summer, and I am still apologizing to her for our lack of sensitivity. But God has used this time of testing to strengthen her. Her capacity to love keeps increasing. Also, she loves to play piano, paint, and cook gourmet meals.

Rebecca married an awesome man of God, Chad, who is able to give great hugs to his mother-in-love. They have both served as the youth pastors at Beth Messiah for several years and then as associate pastors. They had built the teen group from seven young people to over twenty in less than a year. Almost every weekend, they had different teens come and eat dinner with them. There have even been several young people who have come to know the LORD through their ministry. At present they are serving as the senior leaders of our Memphis Tikkun congregation, Brit Hadashah.

They gave us a wonderful granddaughter, Layel Sahme, who is seven. They named her after Samuel, and her name reflects the meaning of Samuel's name, "Heard of God." She continues to bring us joy with her keen wit and to amaze us with her sharp mind. She has already memorized seventy Scripture verses! In February 2009 our daughter gave birth to our youngest grandson, Elon, who is now one. Recently our whole family was with us in Israel for two months, and I got a chance to see his first steps.

Our youngest, Simcha, suffered from our depleted emotional energy as she was home with us during her critical teen years. She did not have the benefit of the same family life the older children had during their teen years. Dan and I stopped doing some family traditions, like building a Succah, each year because of the painful memories they would stir up. Simcha also missed out on some significant mother/daughter times in the kitchen, not so much because of my grief, but because of our travels. In her senior year of high school she wrote a paper about the most influential event or turning point in her life. She wrote about Samuel and the effect his death had on her. It was quite profound. At the end of the paper, she wrote, "Samuel gave up his life so that I might gain mine." This statement pretty much sums up the change that has occurred in her life—she has come to life.

Before Samuel's death, she was shy and insecure, but now she has become an outgoing leader instead of a follower. She was my first child to attend a public school. After losing her brother, Simcha felt that life was short and that she wanted to make a difference before it was too late. There were no opportunities to share her faith at her former Messianic Jewish day school. Almost every week, she invited several of her class friends to youth group, though not all wanted to attend.

Tears come to my eyes when I think of the goodness of the LORD in protecting and prospering my daughter during the year following Samuel's death. Can you imagine going from three siblings living at home to no siblings in one year—one died and the other two getting married? Also, she had to move with us away from her home of ten years, and her favorite cat, Precious, got hit by a car... a lot of loss and change! At one point the pain of grief was so great that she seriously thought of suicide. But God mercifully revealed himself to her. He made his great love known to her and insisted that if she did decide to take her life that she would be with him. However, he tenderly told her that he had a purpose for her life and that only she could fulfill it. Simcha wept in the presence of so much love. It turned her life around.

I marvel at Simcha's love for music—singing, playing the flute, dancing, and playing the drums. Before, she struggled to worship, but now worship is in her heart. She has also discovered that she has a talent for painting. When we moved to Israel, Simcha did not want to come live there with us. She said that she wanted to stay in the states with her brother and sister. Her heart seemed resolved not to move with us. However, I knew in my heart that she was called to Israel as I remembered the vision I had of her when she was born. While we were in Israel in 2000, a group of her friends were going with a special outreach/dance group, called Souled Out, to travel throughout Israel. Simcha decided to go along. Within two days, we received a phone call from her, and she excitedly declared that God had called her to Israel. Simcha became a citizen of Israel when we did in 2000 and joined the Israeli army after her graduation from high school in 2002. And now, she has been in Israel for eight years and has become proficient in Hebrew.

Simcha married Jonathan Moore in 2008, and they both live in Maale Adumin outside of Jerusalem. They serve in a sister ministry, Revive Israel, as the leaders of the discipleship training school. Simcha had known Jonathan since childhood, and his parents are leaders in one of our Tikkun congregations. He is a wonderful addition to the family, as he possesses a sense of humor compatible with Dan's. He loves to play board games, put puzzles together, and have deep theological discussions. Best of all, he adores Simcha.

A couple months after Samuel died, Dan's nephew came to live with us. He was a young man in his late twenties at the time. God brought him at just the right time as his presence helped to fill up our empty house. He was a troubled young man, but God took hold of his life and transformed him. He has been like a son to us and was a great comfort to us during this time. His nature is a lot like Samuel's, and we felt that his being with us at that time was a gift from God. At first, he made several statements about how he never wanted to get married. But, over time, he watched our marriage, and he watched Benjamin and Rebecca go through their courtship and marriage process. He changed his mind and fell in love. We soon had another marriage in October of 2000. He and his wife have served us immensely during this season in our life. Their love and friendship have deeply enriched us. They plan to enter full-time ministry as counselors of troubled teens and young people. And then, in August 2004, we were blessed with another "grandson," the fruit of the marriage of this special couple.

Naturally, the siblings of a deceased one feel as if their parents do not love them as much because the parents talk so much about how wonderful the child was that died. I felt this way when my brother died. And so, Dan and I soon learned to temper our words about our great anguish over the loss of Samuel in front of them and saved our deep grieving for when we were alone. However, we shed many tears together as a family, which I believe was healthy. Working all these issues through just took time—and lots of prayer from our friends. When we learned that our main source of comfort was God, it took the pressure off our relationships.

We also encouraged talking about Samuel with the children. It became very healing to talk about all the good times we had together. Our children preferred, however, to do most of their grieving alone or with their friends. I think they were just fighting the same battle Dan and I were fighting. They felt that they couldn't comfort us and that we couldn't comfort them. They did not want to burden us with their pain and did not want to deal with ours. How important it was to remember this dynamic when working through grief as a family. Each member grieved differently. One child did not like to be forced to talk about her pain; another child did like talking. We had to give each other space.

To keep Samuel's memory alive, we worked on a precious scrapbook together commemorating Samuel's abundant life. Also, we created a memorial case of his favorite toys, his baseball glove and bat, his baseballs, roller blades, and other sports equipment. Included in this case were the numerous e-mails, letters, and cards we received from our friends. For a while, the presence of Sam's things brought me comfort, but then it became a very painful reminder of his absence. I think each person has different comfort levels as to how much of the deceased one's belongings should be lying around. I felt like I moved on too quickly in putting away Samuel's things. I wish I had waited a few months before clearing up Samuel's room and dismantling several of his Lego buildings. This act tore at my heart, and later I wished I hadn't done it.

The good news is that our family did remain intact going through the grieving process. We all grew closer together and can now freely talk about Samuel without moving into competition over whose grief is greatest. We are very grateful to God for restoring our family and releasing a deeper joy in us as we embrace life again. I wish I could say that this was made possible because we did everything right. I think that we had the blessing of being the recipient of prayers from all over the world. Even after many years, I still hear of people praying for us and our family.

Faith's Testimony

And without faith it is impossible to please God, because anyone who comes to him must believe that he exists and that he rewards those who earnestly seek him

Hebrews 11:6

More than just my body and emotions was affected by this trauma of loss. My faith in a God who heals was sorely tested too. Much of the theology that I had accepted for years shook under the strain of unfulfilled hope. The promises in God's Word concerning healing and his response to our faith no longer seemed reliable. More prayer ascended for this one small boy than I have ever heard of before in history! Many powerful prayer warriors fought for his life. Surely there was faith the size of a mustard seed. We even packed a suitcase with his clothes to take with us to his funeral services, believing he would be resurrected. But apparently we did not have the faith to raise him up, and I aggressively asked God, "Why?"

Thankfully, my confidence in his goodness and his love for me did not waver much, but I felt quite undone by not knowing how to apply the passages in Scripture that seem to say that health and healing were God's will for his obedient people. For several years, I shrank back from praying for the sick. I did not want to extend myself again and then be let down. Slowly, I have had to put back these foundation blocks one at a time. I even started a journal called "These Things I Know," where I wrote down promises from the Word that I had absolute confidence in. Gradually, this list grew. Yet the truth that brought me through the tragedies I experienced as a teenager brought me through again. All I needed to really know was that God knew what was going on, he was in control, and that he loved me. It was a rendition of the confession "God is good, and his mercy endures forever."

Hebrews 12:2 admonishes us to fix our eyes on Jesus, the author and finisher of our faith. It is by grace that we even have the faith to believe. Saving faith and resurrection faith come from the LORD. I came to understand that I could confess Scripture until

I was blue in the face yet never obtain healing faith. It was God who opened my eyes so that the written word became rhema. "Faith comes by hearing, and hearing by the word of God, but who opens the ears in revelation?" I wondered. I can think that I believe, but something becomes substance in me when I have real faith. That is a gift of God. We are all dependent on God for our faith, and if he doesn't give us faith sufficient to raise the dead, then the dead are not going to get raised. We can only do what we see the Father doing, and if the Father isn't raising the dead at that moment, neither can we.

It still comes down to drawing closer to God in intimacy; in him is all that we need. We only trust those whom we know. I like what Malcolm Webber said in his book *To Enjoy Him Forever*:

> Jesus is the Author and Perfecter of our faith. Our personal experiential knowledge of him and our faith in him are inseparable. Faith that is purely academic, consisting in nothing more than mental assent with scriptural principles that may in themselves be sound, is not authentic faith, and in times of trial and testing it will always fail. A true faith will triumph and abide forever and is only present in the hearts of those who know him, to whom faith is not a requirement nor duty but a privilege.
>
> Webber, 52

Some try to enter into appropriating the promises of the Word through the door of positive confession, without a relational intimacy with God. Many who are not true believers have found that there is a certain power over the body and circumstances through the power of the mind. Many have received healing just through believing in the power of their confessions. We participate in the disciplines of faith (prayer, fasting, good deeds, etc.) not to gain God's favor but because we have already received mercy and have his "ear." In view of God's mercy, we present our bodies as living sacrifices. A legalistic spirit often tries to bargain with God. ("If I pray this much, fast for days, or do this many good deeds, then you have to heal me, prosper me, or protect me.") When God does prosper us, he never wants us to get to the point where we say with pride, "Look what I have done. I am in health because I have confessed every morning that I am healed. I have a large home because of my confessions. Our congregation is prospering because we have prayed and fasted twenty-one days five times this year." Our actions do have a bearing on our lives, but God's mercy is a major ingredient. We must never forget that God is the one who gives us the ability to produce wealth and he is the one who enlightens us through his spirit so we can have faith for healing, protection, etc.

There is only one door through which true faith can enter, and that is the door of intimacy with our LORD. If our faith is not built on our living relationship with God through Jesus (which involves sharing in his suffering and embracing the cross), then when our confessions do not "work," we will be more apt to throw out the Word and declare that it isn't true. We might even stop believing in a good God all together. If Dan's and my faith had rested in our faith to raise Sam from the dead, then we would be in deep trouble. Our faith rested in a loving God whom we do not always understand or need to understand. We are always being challenged in our hearts. Will we love God even when we do not understand and it seems like the promises are not being fulfilled? God wants us to love him for himself… period! *This place of unanswered prayer is indeed a refiner's fire. God promises to heal yet not all are healed. Who can stand in such a place of disparity, yet we worship and praise God in the midst of not knowing why. This is the fire that refines our faith.*

I look at the grace of faith this way. There is a law of gravity that is trustworthy; that is why they call it a law. But if another force, say your hand, stops a ball from falling, then the new law supersedes the law of gravity. In Scripture, we are told that the law of sin and death (gravity) reigns now and through the cross it is overcome by the law of the spirit of life (the hand or another force to overcome the effects of gravity). There is a strong downward pull of death in this world, and it is only the power of a resurrected life that can overcome it. It is only by the grace and mercy of God that we are not all destroyed through sickness or accident. A question that used to trip me up was "Why does anyone fall away from God having known the truth?" until God said I was asking the wrong question. The right question was "How can anyone believe and remain faithful to God?" since we were all bound over to disobedience. In the same way, the question is not "Why are not all those who believe healed?" but "Why are any of us healed to begin with?" Why did Samuel walk away from the hospital when he was age one and not other children in the hospital? A revelation of the abundant grace and mercy of God is the only answer!

Another example we can use concerns a typical interaction with a trustworthy father who promises to take his child to the amusement park on Sunday, and when Sunday comes he backs out because his mother had a stroke. Does this mean that the father doesn't keep his promises? Of course not. A higher value or principle came into play that superseded his promise to the child. He will probably take him at a later date. All promises are subject to the wisdom of God for the moment, as well as for the future.

There is healing faith that glorifies God, and there is overcoming faith (when the promises are not manifest in this life) that glorifies God. We are to always seek healing, but sometimes we fall short for some reason only known by God. It is cruel to judge a person's lack of victory in the area of healing as being a judgment for his or her lack of faith or prayer. *Only God can make such a judgment. It is out of our jurisdiction.*

May our focus not be on whether or not we have enough faith but on whether or not God will be glorified. May there be a greater passion for the LORD's purposes than for our own appropriation of the promises.

Each hero, listed in Hebrews 11, did not receive the things promised before his or her death, yet each person's faith was commended! Each hung in there through suffering because each was living here as a stranger. These heroes loved the giver of the promises more than the promises. The permanence of the unseen world was more desirable than the seen world, which was temporary.

How many of our efforts are self-focused when our true concern should be what will bring God the most glory? I want my life to be modeled after the Apostle Paul, who burned with the heart of God to see life come to those who were lost, even if it meant the personal discomfort of suffering. Yet he moved in such power that the life that was in him was able to be transferred to a handkerchief, which when laid on someone brought healing (Acts 19:11–12). He was for life, yet he willingly gave up his life. He submitted to being stoned, whipped, beaten, spat upon, and without food or sleep, because he was driven with this heart. He counted his life as nothing that he might finish the task set before him. (See Acts 20:22–24.) His concern was that the Messiah would be glorified in his body whether he lived or died. (See Philippians 1:20–24.)

It seems like this issue of faith keeps being an issue about the glory of God. We all have different testimonies, and each one brings glory to God. Since Dan and I had touched many lives through the years of our ministry, many lives were also affected by this tragedy. One of the foremost concerns in all of our friends' hearts was How are Dan and Patty doing? When they saw our lives and faith being strengthened through our suffering, they became encouraged. We had experienced the unthinkable, the loss of a child, yet God's grace was sufficient to bring us through triumphantly. There is a testimony of God's grace that is ongoing in the lives of those who have suffered and have not received what was promised. Madam Guyon was such a person. She inspired many by her writings with the insights she received while in the midst of her sufferings. If she had been healed or if nothing bad ever happened to her, where would the blessing of her books be? Or how about Joni Erickson-Tada? If Joni were healed from her paralysis, would God still be getting glory from her ongoing testimony of the goodness of God to sustain her? She is a living testimony, a living martyr, who is releasing life to all who come in contact with her.

There are different kinds of glory—who is to dictate to God which kind is better? In Romans 9, we read how God received glory out of hardening Pharaoh's heart so as to release the Israelites from bondage: "I raised you up for this very purpose, that I might display my power in you and that my name might be proclaimed in all the earth" (Romans 9:17). "But this isn't fair," you might say. "How can God blame us if he wills something and it comes to pass?" But who are we to question God and talk back to him? "What if God, choosing to show his wrath and make his power known, bore with great patience the objects of his wrath—prepared for destruction? What if he did this to make the riches of his glory known to the objects of his mercy, whom he prepared in advance for glory?" (Romans 9:22–23). It is both faith in God's Word as well as a moment-by-moment revelation of God's will in particular situations that will determine how we are to pray and act. We are partners with God.

Additionally, there is the glory God received when he raised Lazarus from the dead, or healed the blind man, or cast out demons. God received glory through healing me, Samuel, and members of our congregation. Who can understand? Triumphant, overcoming faith (no matter whether the promises are obtained in this life or not) daily brings glory to God and testifies to the riches of his abundant grace, though generally the interpretation of the kingdom of God is to believe for healing and deliverance.

During the battle for faith to raise Sam from the dead, God chose not to give us resurrection faith. We were prophetically told to stand for his resurrection, and that we did with great power. Men and women of different denominations joined us. Never had I seen such unity and courage as more than forty leaders and numerous intercessors stood with us praying over Samuel's lifeless body. Many of us expected to see his little body move; that was how strong our faith was. Yet he left his body and went to heaven. One would think that we lost the battle; however, for a few years afterward, we received (and still are receiving) testimonies of people who attended the services who said their faith was strengthened and not weakened. Something powerful transpired in the lives of over 1,200 people who attended. Many said that they would never be the same. Through natural eyes it looked like death won, but through spiritual eyes it was plain to see that life triumphed!

I have come to the conclusion that it is both faith in God's Word, as well as a moment-by-moment revelation of God's will in particular situations that will determine how we are to pray and act. We are partners with God. Our job is to obey, being empowered by the grace of God, and God's responsibility is to determine the outcome. The glory that is then produced in us becomes a testimony to the faith with which he gifted us.

Healing—Identifying with Jesus

I want to know Christ and the power of his resurrection and the fellowship of sharing in his sufferings, becoming like him in his death, and so, somehow, to attain to the resurrection from the dead.

Philippians 3:10–11

I desire for others to gain hope and encouragement from glimpsing my grief journey. The road to healing isn't linear but more cyclical or up and down in nature. It was gradual and not all at once. Often, I would experience the same stages of moving from pain, to comfort, to healing, and then getting back into embracing life again. I found that identification with the suffering of Jesus was repeatedly a factor in the healing of my pain of loss. It took place a layer at a time.

When the Israelites in the wilderness looked upon the bronze snake on the pole, they were healed from their snake bites. Much in the same way, in my own life, when I looked upon Jesus and thought of his suffering on the cross, I was healed.

Sometimes, a wound has to be lanced before it heals. Samuel's death dredged up all the past junk in my life that still remained unhealed. It was as if the LORD blew the control lid off, and I could no longer keep unresolved issues from affecting me. Instead of just experiencing the pain of past grief, I experienced the pain of past conflicts with parents, husband, children, and past losses. Dan had to deal with unresolved grief over the passing of his father (he died when Dan was nine) and the tormenting thoughts of doubt and unbelief left over from college days when he had the nervous breakdown. But actually, the noticeable healing began in January 1999, when I hit bottom. When you hit bottom there is only one way to go from there, right? Up!

When I was at my lowest, God was the closest. The Word says that God is near the brokenhearted and those who are contrite of spirit. Even though I did not feel all those "goose bumps" of glory-type experiences, I felt the comfort of having his arms about me. I sensed him telling me that the reason I couldn't "see" his face was that he had buried my face in his chest. When you are that close, guess what you hear? His heartbeat.

One time when I walked past Sam's memorial case we kept in the basement, I grabbed hold of his gray baseball shirt (the one he wore to his last game) and pressed it to my chest. I fell to the ground and wailed loudly and pitifully. At that point, I felt carried into the heavenly counsel of Jesus's heart. I began to experience his sorrow over my loss, and I felt him grieving with me. He was telling me that he was sorry that I had to go through this pain. I then felt his suffering over the pain of others all over the world. Soon, I was no longer crying over my loss but grieving over his pain. I then wept over the pain I had caused him when I turned my back on him and chose other "lovers." Instead of always thinking of how things affected me, I started to be concerned about how my actions affected God. This life, after all, is about God, not me. What a different perspective to take on.

How important it was to take the time to heal properly. I had to learn to lean into the pain instead of trying to escape it. Gradually God dealt with more of my manifestations of fear and trauma. This came about as I pressed intently into his throne room. I can remember the last greatest breakthrough came when I found myself at the end of my rope once again. It happened five years after Samuel died, when I had experienced the last in the series of painful events in my life. Even though most of this story is about how I dealt with the loss of Samuel, the completion of my healing process over his death did not happen until this time in my life (though there is still a scar that hurts when rubbed). New painful events in my life opened wide the wound of grief, and the unresolved issues came tumbling down upon me. It occurred at the time of the birth of Rebecca's first child. At one point Rebecca's labor got so intense that she screamed out, "Jesus!" She did not cry out, "Mom," or "Chad," or "Dad" but called out to the only One who could give her strength. It was a cry that came from the depth of her being. But suddenly there was the joy of seeing that precious little baby making her debut into the world. Our hearts erupted with shouts of joy and tears. All the pain was worth it.

When I got home, I listened to the tape of the birth of our son Samuel. At one point in my labor I too cried out to God. Then, when the baby was finally born, I burst into tears of joy. Whenever I listened to this tape in the past, I would always cry at the moment of his birth. But this time, there was grief mingled with the joy as I remembered that morning so long ago. This prepared me for an experience I was to have that following day. Something happened, and new pain was unleashed as I rode off in the car to visit my daughter. I began to shake. I was so hurt and felt like I could no longer endure the level of pain I had been asked to carry all these years. If God did not do something, I knew I was going to die. I let out a scream to top all screams. I cried out from the depth of my being. I called on the name of Jesus with all my heart. It was like I knew in every cell of my body that God was the only One who could deal with all my pain. It was like ultimate faith in operation … raw faith! He came down, into my car, and lifted the years of pain, fear, and grief from me! He set me free, and I burst into tears of joy. God sits on the throne, and he loves me!

God showed me the reason why he had to bring me through all these trials all these years. He was preparing me for Israel as he needed a vessel who would not be intimidated by all the pain and suffering resident in this ancient people. He birthed in me the treasure of knowing that Jesus is the only one sufficient to answer all the pain of loss. After God brought me these words of comfort in the car, I looked up and saw a van with the words written on it "Dr. Comfort." I had graduated from being a nurse to comfort people's souls to being a doctor of comfort! (I have written more extensively of this revelation in a new book called *The Cry*.)

Most of these symptoms of trauma are gone now—but not all. There is still some resident hypertension when things drop or something suddenly moves, but this is nothing compared to what I have been set free from!

Many said to me in the early days that time heals, but at first, I refuted the statement. Many parents who have lost children told me that the pain never goes away, that time does not heal. In some ways, that is true. A person who loses an arm will always know the loss, though he or she might rarely think about it. But, as time did pass, I found that God does heal and restore when you yield to him. In the midst of suffering, it felt like I would never stop hurting, but I have good news—it is not hopeless. When I lost my brother in a car accident along with my best girlfriend so many years ago, I grieved intensely for six months. It felt like the pain would never go away, but then God miraculously took the grief away.

Today, I experience little or no pain when I think of my mother. Rather, I am filled with joy when I think of her being in heaven with Samuel and her being reunited with her son David, whom she waited thirty years to see again! And now, God has removed almost all grief from my loss of Samuel.

Rarely do I weep now, though many times I have tried when I have experienced a longing to see him and hug him. Occasionally, I may go a day or two feeling the old heaviness of grief and the piercing pain of loss. God keeps redirecting my thoughts toward him and usually brings me deeper revelation of himself as I come through the valley. He has also kept me occupied with writing, painting, making jewelry, and loving on my children and grand-children. He has privileged me to travel with Dan all over the world preaching the good news of the God of Israel who never breaks his covenant of love with his people. I do have the power to control what I think about, and I choose to think on the many blessings that have come my way.

I want to encourage you; God has the power to take away your sorrow and turn it into joy. Oh, for the grace to trust him for his perfect timing. Through the power of his grace we do overcome depression. It is not endless. There is hope. Look up, for your redemption is drawing near! Remember, God subjected his creation to frustration in hope. Hope is part of our DNA! One day, all of creation will be covered with the manifest glory of God. For now, let him heal you as you have become identified with him through suffering.

Love's Agony

How great is the love the Father has lavished on us, that we should be called children of God! And that is what we are! The reason the world does not know us is that it did not know him.

1 John 3:1

It seems like more than a coincidence that I prophesied about the love of God the day before the fire. So it comes as no surprise that I was sorely tested in my trust in God's love for me. You and I are the apple of his eye. Such love does the Father have for us that he sent his son to die for us that we might once again come into an intimate relationship with him. It only stands to reason then that God's enemy, Satan, would try to attack those whom he loves most: Us.

When something tragic happens, when something comes in that shakes our very foundations, when a cloud of silence comes in where the heavens are as brass and God's Word is dead to us, a voice as real as our own comes in and tells us that God must not love us. Satan tries our entire lives to get us to doubt God's love and to eventually get us to separate from God, turning our backs on him. He stands to accuse us and tells us that the reason why we feel distant from God is because we did something wrong. That voice bombards our inner being, sometimes to the point where it feels like we cannot even catch our next breath. We are tempted to give up on our quest for knowing God, but somehow we cannot. The spirit of death with the hoards of hell comes in like a flood, like vultures preying on a weak victim, to steal our hearts from the one who truly loves us. This battle for our hearts is the greatest proof that God loves us.

Satan seems to know that there is a torment for me worse than the emotional pain of losing Samuel, and that is the pain of not sensing God's presence. I have often said that I can go through anything as long as I have an ongoing intimacy and fellowship with God. So what is my Achilles' heel? You guessed it—God's silence, his apparent distance. Knowing this, it seems that I would be alert to where the enemy will seek to attack me on a continual basis, putting over my spirit a blanket of death to make me feel separated from God. Oh, to take heart in God's Word, which says that nothing will ever separate me from God's love, the very scripture I read the day before the fire.

> Who shall separate us from the love of Christ? Shall trouble or hardship or persecution or famine or nakedness or danger or sword? As it is written: "For your sake we face death all day long; we are considered as sheep to be slaughtered." No, in all these things we are more than conquerors through him who loved us. For I am convinced that neither death nor life, neither angels nor demons, neither the present nor the future, nor any powers, neither height nor depth, nor anything else in all creation, will be able to separate us from the love of God that is in Christ Jesus our LORD.
>
> Romans 8:35–39

The pain of separation from my son sometimes is so great that it surpasses human comprehension. If I could hurt so much over my loss, how much more grief does God experience over our separation from him? Unbelievers, and even some who call themselves believers, become cut off from the love of God through their unbelief and hardness of heart. It is love that is grieved. Such a great revelation—God is grieved. His love sometimes goes unrequited, and he is sorrowful.

This revelation of the Holy Spirit's sensitivity makes me acutely aware of how important it is to be always yielding to his love in me. Because of my growing love for his work in my life, I hate to cause him grief—because I know what grief feels like. We are even admonished in the Word not to grieve the Holy Spirit. Excerpts from my first two journal entries after the tragic fire illustrate this truth so clearly.

8 July '98

> Death… cold… cut off. When you hug death, the hug does not return to you. It does not weep when you weep; it does not laugh when you laugh. When you speak, it does not lis-

ten; it does not respond. When you say arise, it does not obey. Death… the opposite of life… of love. You know when you pass from death to life when you love one another. A dead person cannot love, cannot feel, and cannot respond. Samuel is gone. His body cannot laugh or cry, smile or frown. It was cold. No warmth. He was taken away, and I cannot go to him. Yet, he was cut off, separate from me. Oh, the agony of unrequited love. Something was ripped from me. Death entered my senses and pierced my soul. The breath of life was stolen from me. You know when you have passed from life to death when you cannot love. Love must find an expression. It is love that is grieved when a life is cut off. It is broken fellowship. There is separation. Love is alive.

God's love is everlasting. We love because he first loved us. Grieve not the Holy Spirit God admonishes us through his Word. We grieve the Holy Spirit when we cut ourselves off from his love through the hardening of our hearts through unbelief. The wages of sin is death—separation. For God so loved the world that he gave his life blood to purchase us so that we may have life. He took death into himself so we may no longer have to fear death. He came so that we might have life and have it more abundantly. God's love has conquered; it is powerful. No man can fathom the depths and the riches of his glorious grace.

Oh, the agony of God's heart that loves with perfect, unconditional love. He does not recoil and protect himself when his love is rejected. He keeps on loving even though we "die" to him. The greatest pain is not the pain I feel over the loss of Samuel—not the trauma of seeing his little body with the flesh burned and falling off, not the horror of him being stuck in a house ablaze with a fiery inferno, not the pain of being helpless, powerless to lift a finger to rescue him—but the pain of loss God experiences every time he has to assign someone to the eternal flames.

Samuel was gone yet I could not go to him. He is our prized jewel, our joy, and our light. Can anyone know the agony? Yes, God does, for his agony is much greater than anything I have experienced. The separation he experiences when someone is sent to hell is permanent, not just a temporary loss like mine.

Can anyone come close to understanding his grief? We are so familiar with how sin affects us, but do we know what happens to the heart of God when we sin?

Because his love is shed abroad in our hearts, it must be allowed to express itself through our loving others with his love. When we love one another, his love is made complete, but, when we do not love, it grieves him. We shut down the flow to life (love) because of fear. Now it seems that fear is more powerful than love. Fear is contagious, and there will be a reign of terror in these last days. Men will hide in caves in fear, the book of Revelation says. But the Word says that perfect love will cast out fear. Jesus is returning for a bride who is manifesting and reflecting the love of her husband. For it will be said of them, "Behold, how they love one another." They will know we are Jesus's disciples when we love one another. The world will come to the knowledge of the glory of God through his glorious love ablaze in his bride. Jesus came to destroy him who has the power of death—that is the devil— and free those who all their lives were held in slavery by their fear of death. We have not received the spirit of fear but of love, of sonship that cries out, "Abba, Father." Death has been swallowed up by victory.

This connection between sin and separation from God continued to be magnified to me as time went on. I began to see how much God hates death, as death is ultimately separation from him. The only death that truly has eternal impact is separation from God as a result of our disobedience. Love is such a manifestation of life and connects people in loving relationships, the very opposite of what sin does. My own suffering united me with Jesus's suffering heart of love manifested at the cross. This ultimate sacrifice forever is a force that works to bind people together. God is the author of life and not death or pain and suffering. We are challenged on a regular basis to embrace the goodness and love of God in the face of the paradox of unanswered prayers. However, God's character does not change in the midst of our pain. He is always there loving us.

9 July '98

The glory of God is in his life—divine love always linked to life. Jesus's love for the Father gave him strength to obey and go to the cross. It was love that compelled him to suffer for our sake. It was the power of love that resurrected him from the dead. We know what it is like to have death touch our body, soul, and spirit. When we experience a death of a loved one, we must keep death from piercing our spirit. Death pierces our body and soul, but our spirit (his spirit linked with our spirit) must triumph. Job was tempted by his wife to curse God and die, but he refused and chose life.

T. Austin-Sparks so beautifully expounds on this revelation of the power of death. He has such a revelation of how sin affects our souls.

> When we commit sin, or are sinned against, death enters our soul. If you touch anything that is other than love—if you touch hate, animosity, suspicion, prejudice, criticism, jealousy, envy, or any other thing that is contrary to love—you touch death. It is horrible. When you meet somebody who is eyeing you, not sure of you, suspicious of you, oh how helpless, how hopeless the situation is; you cannot get on, you are glad when you have passed, but you are sad. You have met with a touch of death. You touch love in another child of God coming out to you, and oh, what a prospect fills the air, what possibilities arise! You have touched life when you touch love.
>
> *His Great Love* by Sparks, 80

> The tree of life is for those who love with God's love. We need people to love us but also others need our love. We will not enlarge the other person's life by criticizing him or eyeing him. In the garden, man failed to reciprocate the love of God and doubted and questioned and disbelieved and disobeyed—all of which is contrary to love—therefore man was forbidden to partake of divine life and faded like a flower. That life was essential for God's purpose but it was lost on the ground of lost love, failure in love.
>
> *His Great Love* by Sparks, 76

God knew how much Samuel's death would hurt me, yet he allowed it. Again we are confronted with the mystery of causation and understanding the word discipline. Could it be that what I went through in this hardship hurt him more than it hurt me? What a thought! It cannot be! It would be like me killing my grandchild (though I am using this analogy it does not adequately explain the mystery of who or why), knowing the devastation and confusion it would cause my son or daughter-in-law and then telling them to trust me. This kind of love surpasses my human understanding. As I try to grasp it, I am overcome with fear and wonder with thanksgiving. How could he endure the pain? He endured for the joy set before him... a bride fashioned for his son... a bride without spot or wrinkle who made herself beautiful like the godly women of old by quietly trusting the wisdom of her Father.

The Apostle Paul endured because he saw, in a glorious but awesome vision on the road to Damascus, the one whom he was persecuting. To behold him is to love him. Such love so captured his heart that he endured beatings, stonings, shipwrecks, famine, and danger all day long. Why? He saw the love the Father had for his son. He took up that same love for him and fell in love with his purpose—to fashion a bride to rule by his side for eternity.

Such a mystery is this love. One time, I tried to get Samuel in touch with the anger he had buried inside of himself as a result of an early childhood trauma. I sat him down with my pencil and paper, as I often would do, and began to draw pictures of his hospital experience. I showed him as an infant all tied down with IVs strapped to both his wrists and his ankles. Then I drew a picture of me standing by his bed with him looking at me. I asked him how this would make him feel. He said it would make him feel angry. (So far, so good. He was getting the point!)

I then acted out with him how I had to feed him four different kinds of medicine four times a day. I put him in my lap and strongly restrained him with my arms and legs so he could not move. Then, I pretended to squirt medicine down his throat. He began to struggle and struggle, as he hated to be restrained. "How does this make you feel?" I asked him. He said, "Angry!" He was making all the right responses!

Next I explained how he was too little to understand the doctor's intentions—he did not want to hurt him. The doctor just wanted to make Samuel feel better, but in the process of doing this, he had to cause him pain. Also, because I loved him, I had to let the doctor hurt him, and I had to restrain him to give him medicine that would make him better. It also pained me terribly, knowing he was hurting. I asked him, "Why do you think I let you hurt so much?"

"Because you love me so much and did not want me to die," he said. I went on to say that it was hard for him to trust me because of what had happened to him, but that was okay because he was too little to know we were not out to do him harm. Then, his little eyes lit up (he was about eleven years old at the time) when he looked over at the picture of himself as a baby tied down on the hospital bed. He exclaimed, "I was just like Isaac, who was tied down on the altar by his father, but Isaac wasn't angry because he trusted his father. He knew that his father would do nothing that would really be bad for him." My eyes filled with tears as the Holy Spirit revealed this to my son. I had originally planned to give this illustration to Samuel, but the Holy Spirit beat me to it. Do I have that kind of trust in my loving Father? Do you?

Such a paradox I experienced, to go through the worst time in my life and yet gain a deeper understanding of God's great love for me. I came to understand that everything that happens to us can be explained in terms of God's love. We need supernatural strength to comprehend the width, breadth, and depth of God's love. (See Ephesians 3:14–19.)

Once when Dan and I were in Turkey, shortly after Samuel died, we toured the estate of one of the richest sultans. Several rooms in this opulent palace contained numerous priceless treasures. I never saw so many rubies, emeralds, gold, pearls, and diamonds in my life. The treasure was so vast that viewing the jewels became mundane after a while. Dan and I looked at each other and asked ourselves if we were given a choice between all this wealth and the life of Samuel, what would we choose? In an instant, we both said "Samuel." For God so loved the world that he gave the best of all he had to purchase us. He chose us!

On the morning of the fire, I went into the burning house to try to rescue the children. The heat and smell overcame me. How powerless I was to save. Yet we have one who loves us so much that he sent his son into the burning inferno to set the captives free. Through the power of a resurrected life, he conquered death so that we might live. No greater love does a man have than this, that he lay down his life for his friend!

For months after the fire, I had difficulty singing songs about the fire of God. People would often loudly declare how they wanted the fire of God to consume them or wanted revival fire to fill their church. Did they know the power and pain of fire? Sometimes I would break down and cry and could not sing. At one conference, they even had a song, "There is fire in the house." This came too close to home, and I shrank back in fear. But it was at this conference that God spoke to me through Isaiah 54.

> "See, it is I who created the blacksmith who fans the coals into flame and forges a weapon fit for its work. And it is I who have created the destroyer to work havoc; no weapon forged against you will prevail, and you will refute every tongue that accuses you. This is the heritage of the servants of the LORD, and this is their vindication from me," declares the LORD.
>
> Isaiah 54:16–17

He revealed to me that even in the burning house, his love was in operation—that his character of goodness and love did not diminish in the midst of this trial. God's character of love did not change the morning of the fire. He is always the same. There was nowhere on this planet that I could go to escape his love. His love did not stay outside the house and wait until the children or I came out in order to manifest itself again. He was there to uphold me when I could not reach Samuel—I felt his presence. He was with me at the funeral when he enabled me to dance. I experienced his love the numerous times he came through with comfort when I cried out to him. He manifests his love every time I get a chance to share my testimony to another hurting parent. And the love that Dan and I have for each other is just another proof that God's love is being released again and again. Oh, love's agony that was expressed for us and that we now can express to others.

Restful Reliance

These are the words of him who is holy and true, who holds the key of David. What he opens no one can shut, and what he shuts no one can open. I know your deeds. See, I have placed before you an open door that no one can shut. I know that you have little strength, yet you have kept my word and have not denied my name.

Revelation 3:7–8

We do not want you to be uninformed, brothers, about the hardships we suffered in the province of Asia. We were under great pressure, far beyond our ability to endure, so that we despaired even of life. Indeed, in our hearts we felt the sentence of death. But this happened that we might not rely on ourselves but on God, who raises the dead.

2 Corinthians 1:8–9

Though I cannot say that God directly causes sickness and hardships, I can say that his redemptive power is so complete that much good can come out of the suffering. So much so that it looks as though God has caused it, for why else have I reaped so much fruit? One of the main aspects of suffering, as I see it from the Word and my own experience, is that it makes us weak so that we come to rely upon God's strength and not our own. Therefore, it is no surprise that trauma serves this purpose, in that it reduces a person to a state of powerlessness. Trauma produces a brokenness that even causes one to despair of life itself. Brokenness is one of the blessed fruits of suffering!

Often, we think we have come to the end of ourselves when in reality we haven't, just because we equate being emotionally a wreck with coming to the end of self. But the evidence of having come to the end of self is a ceasing of striving and is a coming into a place of rest. All it takes is one brick wall you cannot remove, you cannot climb, or you cannot go under. The wall may come upon you suddenly, such as in a loss, or it may be built up slowly as in the waiting of a fulfillment of a promise. This can be seen in the life of Moses (who was a shepherd for forty years before fulfilling his life's call) or in the life of Joseph (who waited years in slavery and prison for his dreams to come true) or in the life of Abraham (who became as good as dead as he waited for the promised child). All these men came to the conclusion that if these promises were going to be fulfilled, God was going to have to fulfill them. The promise became the immovable wall to them. These walls break us and become the cross to self, but complete breaking takes longer.

The Holy Spirit, in order to bring us to a point of usefulness, erects these walls as agents of breaking. Through the cross, we come to a fuller knowledge of God that cannot be gained through just studying the Word.

We must be prepared "to let the cross be so applied in [our] life that [we] are broken and emptied and fairly ground to powder—so [we] are brought to the place where, if the LORD does not do something, [we] are finished" (*Prophetic Ministry* by Sparks, 78). God draws near to those who are contrite in spirit, to those who have allowed the work of the cross to break them so that the LORD's life is released to flow out.

When Samuel died, my life came to an abrupt halt. I found myself in a situation where there was no hope for human intervention. Samuel's body was dead and buried, and I could not go back and reverse the situation, though how often I have rehearsed that fatal decision over and over again. I wish I had never let him spend the night at the neighbors, but I was powerless to change anything. There was no changing the situation, so the only thing that could change was me. I had to find some strength to go on, and God was the only place to go. Something happens to a person when he or she has no place else to go but to God. There no longer is any double-mindedness. I knew beyond all shadow of a doubt that no one or no thing could help me. To whom do I go, only he has the words of life? All other roads led to a suffering without hope.

During other crises in my life, I have learned the power of pressing in, but never had I pressed in like this. When you press in and press into God, you begin to take on his image. It is a certainty. If you press your hand onto a rough surface, and you press long enough and hard enough, your hand will eventually take on the impression of the surface of the object. When we press into God for a short season it is like we have stopped squeezing the rough object too soon and wonder where the imprint is. Being conformed into the image of Jesus takes time and is often painful. Such is the process of breaking I went through.

As long as a person thinks he can manage (control) his own life, he will continue to do so. Such a person has not come to the end of his self-life, nor has he allowed himself to be broken by his wall.

Pain avoidance (I am talking about the pain coming from personal loss or conflict) retards one's spiritual growth, and one misses the blessing God wants to give out of the breaking. Trials and sufferings work to perfect some believers and work to destroy others. The same fire (trials) that tempers the blade of the sword also melts and consumes other metals. The pressure within the ground transforms some wood into coal that will brightly burn as a testimony to the author of its transformation, while it also crushes another type of wood into dust. We are tested and refined through our trials, and our choices determine whether we are consumed or transformed.

I like how Webber sums this up in his book, *To Enjoy Him Forever*:

> God's intention in allowing the trial is that you abandon all hope and trust in your own strength, and in your own ways, and in the things of this life to sustain you, and throw yourself more completely upon Jesus and his wonderful grace. If you will, in this way, submit yourself to your faithful creator, rejoicing in whatever he allows to come your way, knowing it is all for your ultimate greater participation in his glory, then you will have learned the meaning of your life upon the earth.
>
> Webber, 133

God is too big for me to move him against his will. He isn't changing, so guess what that means? I am the one that has to move. Unless God builds a house, we labor in vain. In some ways, what I have been through was easier than what others go through where they still have a way out. I had no way out. It was as plain as the nose on my face. Maybe in these other situations it is not so obvious that there really is no way out. It just looks that way. In this experience, I rejoice. God has made a way and is smashing my other "control" mechanisms.

God is in ultimate control, and the sooner we come to this realization, the sooner we can come into his rest. If we don't, we are fighting a losing battle. I have grown in my awe of the LORD's wisdom to the extent that I would not dare do anything under my own initiative. I want to get to the point where I only do what I see my Father doing, in the same way Jesus walked out his obedience. I am not there yet. How will I know when I have been completely broken?

> One is not broken until all resentment and rebellion against God and man is removed. One who resents, takes offense, or retaliates against criticism and opposition or lack of appreciation is unbroken. All self-justification and self-defense betrays an unbroken spirit. All discontent and irritation with providential circumstances and situations reveals unbrokenness. Genuine brokenness usually requires years of crushing, heartache, and sorrow. Thus are self-will surrendered and deep degrees of yieldedness and submission developed, without which there is little agape love.
>
> *Don't Waste Your Sorrows* by Paul Billheimer, 75

Death to self means knowing what is my responsibility, what is God's responsibility, and what is another's responsibility. I went through great torment as a wife, mother, and pastor's wife. I felt that it was my responsibility to protect myself, my children, my husband, and our congregants from experiencing pain or to relieve their pain. Because this task proved impossible, I would often go around feeling like an absolute failure. To make matters worse, others blamed me when I was not able to deliver—such a vicious cycle! But then God showed me that avoidance of pain was not the goal because God often uses pain to break people of their self-sufficiency. By stepping in and taking over, I was actually hindering God from having his way with others and was imparting to them the same fear of pain that I had. Rather, bringing people to Jesus was my true responsibility. He was the one that was responsible to bring resolution to their pain. I could then act as a midwife to encourage the sufferer to keep pressing into God until he had his way and something was birthed in his or her life. This understanding took a big load off my shoulders.

Also, in confronting my limitations, I came to understand that only God had the power to will something and have it done just the way he willed it. Not everything I "willed" came to pass—only God had that power. These thoughts have comforted me and have relieved me of a lot of unwanted anxiety and stress. Why "will" something that is not God's will? It is a waste of my time and energy!

Another evidence of being broken by the wall was that I didn't exert energy in much futile thinking. I seemed to know not to go down certain roads, as I had been there before and knew where they led—nowhere. Why bother wasting your emotional energy on that which is not profitable? I had had enough emotional expenditure this past year, and now it was necessary for me to rest. When I injured my back several years ago, I knew not to lift up heavy objects because greater injury could occur to my back. In the same way, picking up heavy emotional objects, for a broken person, could cause greater injury and impede the healing process.

We are on the road to wholeness all our lives, and we must learn to keep our emotions freed up so that God may be released to do his part—such an easier way! May God continue to work in my life to break me of picking up unnecessary emotional baggage. I hope I do not have to run into too many more walls before he has completed the process of breaking in me, but not my will. It's restful reliance that I want more of in my life!

God's Hidden Riches in Jesus

My purpose is that they may be encouraged in heart and united in love, so that they may have the full riches of complete understanding, in order that they may know the mystery of God, namely, Christ, in whom are hidden all the treasures of wisdom and knowledge.

Colossians 2:2–3

Brokenness leads to transformation—transformation into the image of Jesus. Coming to the knowledge of Jesus is the best fruit that comes from suffering, for in seeing (knowing) him, you become like him.

About a month after the death of Samuel, I attended a conference in Virginia sponsored by Robert Stearns, Joanne McFadder, and others. Dan and I felt completely devastated, vulnerable, and empty. We wanted so much to be refreshed at the conference, but receiving anything from the LORD proved difficult. The wall of grief blocked my ability to concentrate, yet God's faithfulness broke through, and Jesus became even more precious to me.

During one of the sessions, God impressed upon my heart different scriptures about stones of remembrance. For example, after the prophet Samuel cried out to the LORD on behalf of Israel, the LORD supernaturally delivered them from the Philistines. He took a stone and placed it between Mizpah and Shen and said, "Thus far the LORD has helped us" (1 Samuel 7:7–12). Being led of the spirit, I went outside and picked up a "stone of remembrance" for me to hold. During worship times at the remainder of the conference, I tightly held the stone inside my clenched fist as if it represented life to me. It felt like I held onto the only stone left after the building of my life had blown up. I pictured myself sitting on the floor rocking back and forth with only one block left in my hands. That block (stone) was Jesus, the chief cornerstone. In him, all the promises are yes and amen. In him, dwells all that I need to go on. He became my rock that day as I gripped that stone and cried out to him. The truth about the certainty of his character took root deep within me. Jesus was my rock of salvation!

In the midst of the tempest, I found that my anchor held. My life had totally turned upside down—even my theology and purpose. Everything about my family, congregational family, and me had changed. Nothing would ever be the same again as everyone who knew Samuel was affected, yet there was one who never changes … and that is Jesus. Do you have any idea how comforting the thought was that there exists a reality that never changes? Oh, how I grabbed that stone even tighter. I am so grateful for this one truth: Jesus is the same yesterday, today, and tomorrow. Everything that could be shaken was shaken, but I received a kingdom, and am receiving a kingdom, that can never be shaken! Such worship erupted from my spirit in utter thankfulness. This scripture took on new meaning.

> At that time his voice shook the earth, but now he has promised, "Once more I will shake not only the earth but also the heavens." The words "once more" indicate the removing of what can be shaken—that is, created things—so that which cannot be shaken may remain. Therefore, since we are receiving a kingdom that cannot be shaken, let us be thankful, and so worship God acceptably with reverence and awe, for our "God is a consuming fire."
>
> Hebrews 12:26–29

When everything around me was shaking, Jesus was the anchor that kept my soul from collapsing from the weight of grief. His faithfulness held me close even when I was weak and in despair. I love this old hymn that I used to sing as a little child. Such is the assurance we have in God.

My Anchor Holds
Though the angry surges roll
On my tempest driven soul,
I am peaceful, for I know,
Wildly though the winds may blow,
I've an anchor safe and sure
That can evermore endure.
Mighty tides about me sweep,
Perils lurk within the deep,
Angry clouds o'er shade the sky,
And the tempest rises high;

Still I stand the tempest's shock,
For my anchor grips the rock.
Griefs like billows o'er me roll;
Tempters seek to lure astray;
Storms obscure the light of day:
But in Christ I can behold,
I've an anchor that shall hold.

(W.C. Martin and Daniel B. Towner, 1902)

The words of this great hymn bring such comfort. So many saints long ago understood; they were acquainted with grief. Yes, their anchor held, and by God's grace, my anchor will hold too! The LORD took me places during that conference; I beheld the glory of his son. The baptism of fire came upon me, and I shook violently with this revelation: He is worthy of all our praise and honor. My precious rock is higher than me.

Take comfort with me from these well-known passages of Scripture. They all emphasize the firm foundation we have when our hope and trust is in Jesus.

I love you, O LORD, my strength. The LORD is my rock, my fortress and my deliverer; my God is my rock.

Psalm 18:1–2

He lifted me out of the slimy pit, out of the mud and mire; he set my feet on a rock and gave me a firm place to stand.

Psalm 40:2

From the ends of the earth I call to you, I call as my heart grows faint; lead me to the rock that is higher than I.

Psalm 61:2

He is like a man building a house, who dug down deep and laid the foundation on rock. When a flood came, the torrent struck that house but could not shake it, because it was well built.

Luke 6:48

God is rebuilding my house on a firm foundation, the foundation of his great love found in Jesus. For several years I kept that little stone in my purse and would take it out from time to time. It was a reminder to look to him who is the rock of my Salvation, the one in whom I can put my trust.

Jesus, in whom are hidden all the treasures of wisdom, woos me into his heart. He holds my very next breath. My love for him proved greater than my love for Samuel; praise be to God. The more his love for me unfolds, the more my love for him increases, the more precious the intimacy, and the easier it becomes to live without Samuel. Truly, he heals the brokenhearted!

He has become my comfort, my joy, and my peace. When the storms of emotions overwhelm me, I find refuge under his wings. When I feel like my foot is slipping, he pulls me up to stand on solid ground once again. When the cords of death seek to strangle me, he cries out with authority, "Come forth, Patty. Throw off those grave clothes," and I come to life again. Though I may experience days of darkness still, it doesn't last forever. As I rest in him, he overcomes the darkness with the radiance of his presence. The grace of God knows no limits.

In the beginning, my confidence in God's goodness shook, but now it is strengthened. Such a deep transaction has taken place—more of him and less of me! Through the pain of grief, a veil has been torn in two, and I moved from the holy place into the holy of holies. My life in the flesh was like that curtain in the Temple blocking me from beholding his glory—the greatness of his goodness and love. It had to be torn through suffering; I know no other way. Hebrews 10:20 speaks of Jesus's flesh being the veil that was torn so we might enter into a fuller fellowship with the father. Now I too have become identified with Jesus in this process in order to behold him.

God continually reveals himself from one degree of glory to the next. During the Jewish High Holy Day season of September 1999, my husband was away on a ministry trip. Since Samuel's death, Dan and I have been separated from each other only on a couple of occasions for a few days. This time, he was gone for over ten days. I was particularly despondent during his absence, and this depression seemed to last for over two weeks. I was so used to sitting in his lap whenever I was blue, and now I felt restless because I no longer had this source of comfort. I wondered why God wasn't coming through to comfort me. Desperately, I called out to God, but he was silent. Against my better judgment, I involved myself in too many passive video games and movies and ended up feeling emptier. But then, on Yom Kippur, God broke through.

On Yom Kippur, I took a walk around a nearby lake in our neighborhood. I was seeking the face of my lover—where had he gone? Once again, I found myself questioning the security of my relationship with God. "Have I somehow sinned—here goes that terrible doubting again—and has God's favor lifted? Where can I find comfort today over Sam's death? Does his death still count, and does my pain of loss still affect the heart of God?" I anxiously looked for a sign from heaven of the love of God or something that could be looked at as a message from Samuel, a piece of paper with his name on it, anything. But there seemed to be an impenetrable distance between Samuel and me. I did not like the fact that God would not allow Samuel to at least write a letter or make a phone call.

I knew that on this day it was traditional among the practicing Jews to throw stones into a body of water to signify that their sins are forgiven and removed from them; they are thrown into the depths of the sea and remembered no more. I found two white stones and had a sense that I should throw them into the still pond, and so I did, one at a time. I watched as concentric circles of waves radiated from the point of contact of stone and water. Marveling at the effect that the two little stones made on the surface of the water, I observed that those little ripples kept on going until they reached the edge of the pond. Even though there were two series of concentric circles made from two stones, neither one of their ripples stopped the other from reaching the shore. I felt the spirit of the LORD speak to me, "If a little stone can have such a big impact on a large pond, don't you think the effect of Sam's death will continue in the unseen world until the very end? Notice too how both stones created their own circles of disturbance, and though they became interconnected, each circle of ripple made it to the edge of the pond. Not even a sparrow can fall to the ground without my taking note. Because I am at peace and am surrounded by peace [the water surrounding his throne is a sea of glass (Revelation 4:6)], the slightest disturbance does not go unnoticed, though I myself am forever in peace."

God had met me—he made contact and gave me another treasure of truth about himself. The heaviness lifted. I was assured all over again that my name was written in the Lamb's book of life. God never removed his great love from me. His silence never means separation or aloofness on his part. He forever works to make me press in and press in so I can come to know him and understand that I cannot live without him. He is my treasure hidden in darkness!

Here is another story about this treasure I have found in Jesus. About three years after Samuel died, Dan and I were going through another season of upheaval and pain as we struggled through our relationship with our friends who took over our home congregation. Dan and I were in our car on a ministry trip when I remarked to him about my despair over all the suffering we were going through. I asked him, "Do you really think leadership and life are worth all this suffering?" He did not answer.

That night I had a dream. I dreamed from Revelation 5, where John was giving an account of his vision of heaven and the glory surrounding the throne. The first part of my dream was of a series of acts in a play. I was involved both as an observer and as an actor. Different situations of believers in trials unfolded in each scene. This play was a story of believers overcoming obstacles in the power of God—they were the overcomers written about in Revelation.

At the end of the play, we were all coming to the front of the stage, getting ready for a curtain call, when I heard God's voice. He told me that he wanted to show me what was up ahead. He took me on a journey into some heavenly realm and began to reveal the different aspects of his glory. First, he showed me the glory surrounding his throne. It was quite awesome! Then, I heard him announce the Lion of the tribe of Judah that had triumphed. There was an even greater glory that was displayed. Next, there was almost a holy reverence and worship as I heard a voice declare, "Behold, the Lamb that was slain!" I fell on my face and was undone. Never had I experienced such glory. I then began to cry out, "Yes, it is worth it; it is worth it!" I saw then that all of my questions of "worth" had found its worthiness in this one who was slain from before the foundation of the world. "Worthy, worthy, is the Lamb who was slain." There is a lamb, a slain lamb, sitting in the center of the throne! There is a compassionate God ruling the universe—one who forever identifies with our suffering.

After this, the Lord lifted me up, and with great delight told me that he wanted me to see his bride. He took me to a place on a hill overlooking the scene that was unfolding. He showed me the actors from the play I was in, coming forward toward him. As they came, they all turned into radiant gems and were formed into a beautiful temple, a temple of living stones—perhaps the heavenly Jerusalem that was to come. Again, I fell prostrate and cried out, "Glory!" Such radiance and delight surrounded the heavenly creatures as this bride was revealed. It was as if this was the reason why the whole of creation endured the suffering—it was for the joy set before them. All I could shout was, "Glory!"

Then, he told me that I had to go back and tell the people, the actors of the play, that it is worth it. So, reluctantly, I left his presence and found myself before the crowd of actors. I started to share with them what I saw, and I fell on my face once again. All I could say was, "Glory! Glory! Glory!"

Surpassing Peace

Of the increase of his government and peace there will be no end.
He will reign on David's throne and over his kingdom, establishing
and upholding it with justice and righteousness from that time on
and forever. The zeal of the LORD Almighty will accomplish this.

Isaiah 9:7

After looking over the last few chapters, I have come to see that actually, the fruit that comes from suffering follows the list of the fruits of the spirit found in Galatians and Colossians. Have you ever noticed the kind of peace that you experience after a storm? Everything is calm, and the air feels so clean. Or how about the peace that happens after your three toddlers are finally in bed and you sit down for a cup of tea? These occurrences of peace are nice but conditional to our environment's being at "peace." There is a deeper peace that God wants to bring us. He wants us to be at rest in the midst of storms and chaos and have this peace separate from what happens around us. To accomplish this, God works through our circumstances to break our outer man so we no longer respond to negative external stimuli. A painful process indeed! I found the following excerpts from Watchmen Nee's *The Release of the Spirit* most helpful in expressing these thoughts:

> When the outward man lives in activities, they can disturb the inward man. Thus the outward man is not a helper but a disturber. When the outward man is broken, the inward man enjoys peace before God. Formerly our emotions could be easily aroused, either stirring our love, the most delicate emotion, or provoking our temper, the crudest. But now no matter how many things crowd upon us, our inward man remains unmoved, the presence of God unchanged, and our inner peace unruffled.
>
> Nee, 25

Brokenness, then, does not come by the supply of grace to the inward man but comes by God using external means to decrease our outward man.

It would be well nigh impossible for the inward man to accomplish this, since these two are so different in nature that they can scarcely inflict any wound on each other. Accordingly the nature of the outward man and that of external things are similar; thus the former can be easily affected by the latter. External things can strike the outward man most painfully... Nothing is accidental. God's ordering is according to his knowledge of our needs, and with a view to the shattering of our outward man. Knowing that a certain external thing will thus affect us, he arranges for us to encounter it once, twice, and even more... everything ordered by God for your education.

Nee, 59

When our outer man is broken, we do not need to escape to a quiet place for us to experience peace and the presence of God. We will abide in his presence even when we occupy ourselves with dishes, laundry, bookkeeping, or driving the car. Though outwardly we may be engaging in some activity that is not directing our hearts toward God, our inner man will be fellowshipping with God.

In January and February of 1999, when I reached my lowest point, I experienced a deep restlessness and a violence taking place on the inside of me. I struggled against the "iron bars" that imprisoned me, and I so much wanted to be free. My emotions and my heart condition limited my activity so I could no longer do what I wanted to do. I wanted out of the "straightjacket" I was in. By dint of effort, I was used to accomplishing what I had set my heart on—but then I was powerless. I was tired of all the mourning business, and I wanted life to get back to normal but to no avail. As I went from person to person—even doctor to doctor—in search of the key to unlock the cell, I found myself getting more and more frustrated because no one could help. I soon found that only God had the "I will" that could accomplish what he set his heart on doing.

One day, when I was on a personal retreat, God highlighted a particular passage (Zechariah 9:11–12) to me and said that only he had the key to open the door. The prison was his, and I was a prisoner of hope, not despair. He said that I would have peace as soon as I stopped struggling and accepted his will. The violence I was experiencing was the war going on between my will and his will. Peace would happen when I stopped living my life according to my own understanding and allowed him to live his life in me through the work of the Holy Spirit. I asked myself, "Do I trust him enough to let go completely? Can I view this time of limitation as God's act of mercy in my life?" The words below seemed to answer these questions:

> The restraining ministry of the Holy Spirit restrains us, if we could but see it. For in the restraint he is surely protecting us from a harm we cannot see as we could blindly pursue our own direction... Whenever the LORD restrains, he is actually enfolding you in his protective embrace, not keeping you from what will bring you happiness. His control is really his release in disguise.
> *A God Who Heals the Heart* by Steve Fry, 81

I could look at God's fences as a restriction to keep me from enjoying something I thought was good, or as a protection for me from some harm I could not see. The LORD continued to instruct me and showed me the violence that took place at the cross when the earth quaked and men rose up out of their graves. The hordes of hell had tried all Jesus's life to get him to exert his own will, but they failed. Jesus was faithful to do the will of his Father to the very end and became obedient even unto death... "Not my will," he said, "But Yours be done." He broke free from the law of sin and death. He made it possible for all those following in his footsteps to slay the "dragon." Hence, peace comes by violence.

There is comfort and encouragement in the Word concerning this issue of peace being forged in our lives. One doesn't have to look very far in Old Testament history to find this truth in operation. When Israel would fall into idolatry, God would raise up an army from a neighboring country, and it would defeat Israel in battle and oppress them. After several years of oppression, Israel's cries would reach God, and he would raise up a deliverer among the Israelites who would lead them to victory against their enemy. Then they would have peace until once again their will began to deviate from the will of their heavenly father, and the cycle of oppression, war, and liberty continued.

In the Old Testament, we also find that the kings established peace in their kingdom by getting rid of all the dissidents—killing off all those who disagreed with them. But more importantly, they would have peace when they sought the LORD, encouraged their subjects to seek him, and also got rid of the idols, high places, and foreign altars. Here is one particular scripture that illustrates this point.

> Asa did what was good and right in the eyes of the LORD his God. He removed the foreign altars and the high places, smashed the sacred stones and cut down the Asherah poles. He commanded Judah to seek the LORD, the God of their fathers, and to obey his laws and commands. He removed the high places and incense altars in every town in Judah, and the kingdom was at peace under him. He built up the fortified cities of Judah, since the land was at peace. No one was at war with him during those years, for the LORD gave him rest.
>
> 2 Chronicles 14:2–6

In congregational life, often the way to peace is division, which is dividing off the faction in disagreement with the leadership so that there is one heart and mind in the community. Unfortunately, the peace that is gained by removing those of opposing wills is temporary. Disagreements and wars start because of the war that goes on inside of us. We want something but do not get it (James 4). We have not because we ask not, and if we do ask, we ask amiss. Real peace comes down to there being only one will, and that is the will of the only one who is perfectly just and loving and good.

Peace and freedom go hand in hand. When you become intimately connected to that which is totally free, by laying down your own will, you become one with the movements of the Father. Picture a small child standing on the feet of his father, and the father whisks the child around on the dance floor with expertise and grace. The child doesn't even know how to dance, but that doesn't matter—he is connected to his father who does. He is freed from his own limitations. Similarly, when we are connected to our heavenly Father, we are freed from our earthly limitations, and with God all things become possible. We can be at peace because he is at peace.

A good friend of mine would often comfort me greatly during my hardest months of mourning. She would say that when God healed me of all the trauma I experienced the year our son died, I would enter into a greater peace than I had ever known before. She said that as I learned to trust God through such hard times, every other trouble would seem insignificant. I would be immovable. Everything else pales by comparison. What is dirty laundry, people leaving the congregation, bad hair days, and cranky husbands or children compared with losing Samuel? If God kept me by his grace that fateful year, then I could trust him to keep me through anything I might face in the future.

In times of darkness, of confusion, and of not hearing the voice of God, I learned that it was time to be still. It is so difficult for the human mind to grasp this quietness. I am so geared to doing, to activity, and to solving problems. When the darkness strikes fear in me, I am tempted to run to and fro seeking answers or a way out of the trial. But the darkness often is God's call to me to cease doing. Sometimes he benched me for a while, and if I yielded in these times, the God of peace would put my heart to rest. The sun would soon come out, and I could return to activity, strengthened and refreshed, with a little more revelation of the grace of God.

We don't always get answers to the questions we ask in times of tragedy and hardships. God is often silent. But we have a choice: we can either allow ourselves to struggle and struggle to find answers and eventually get bitter and lose faith, or in these times of silence we can break through to peace by yielding to the wisdom of an infinite God. Peace is the evidence we have submitted our wills to God. Peace never comes on the basis of feeling his presence; otherwise, when we don't feel his presence we will be in turmoil. Steve Fry states this beautifully in his book *A God Who Heals the Heart*:

> If the only way we can be content is to get answers, then are we not actually being ruled by knowledge? If we go a step further and simply ask God for a sense of his presence in our place of need, feeling that the only way we can be content is to know he's there, then are we not being ruled by our senses? If our peace is predicated on these things, it indicates that our submission to God is for what he does, what he gives to us. Yet, there comes a point where we struggle and struggle, turning this way and that, wanting answers, needing supply yet finding again only silence. Why? Because when we finally stop kicking, we enter his peace. That's the rulership God wants us to understand. Beyond his supply, beyond his anointing in your life, beyond his guidance there is peace—the contentment that comes from a trust in God, even when we don't sense him near. Contentment based on these other things suggests a submission to God for what he does; peace, on the other hand, is the evidence that we've submitted because of who he is.
>
> Fry, 107–08

When we are at peace, broken and malleable, we then can be trusted with a treasure of the beautiful radiance of God's spirit. This beauty is not the beauty of outward adornment, but a beauty of a heart at peace—a surpassing peace—because it trusts in a good and loving God. In 1 Peter 3:5, we are told that the women of old used to make themselves beautiful through their reverent submission to their husbands. In the same way, we too will be made beautiful as we reverently submit to our bridegroom.

Beauty from Ashes

The spirit of the Sovereign LORD is on me, because the LORD has anointed me to preach good news to the poor. He has sent me to bind up the brokenhearted, to proclaim freedom for the captives and release from darkness for the prisoners, to proclaim the year of the LORD's favor and the day of vengeance of our God, to comfort all who mourn, and provide for those who grieve in Zion—to bestow on them a crown of beauty instead of ashes, the oil of gladness instead of mourning, and a garment of praise instead of a spirit of despair.

Isaiah 61:1–3

Someone once said, "There are two things that pierce the soul: beauty and affliction." As I reflected on this statement, I recalled an event that happened while Dan and I were in Switzerland on a prayer initiative in September 1997.

While driving to the conference site, I found it hard to take in all the beauty. Never had I seen anything quite like the mountains and lakes, massive rock outcroppings and cliffs of this country. Everything man had touched seemed to perfectly fit in with the ambiance of the natural beauty of what God created—from the Swiss chalets, to the gardens, to the many fenced-in pastures, to the large bells on the cows, which made music whenever the cows moved—everything was perfect. It was as if man had an innate sense of what God had purposed for Switzerland, and they were working in cooperation with God, not against him. What kind of beauty could penetrate my soul to the point where I had to close my eyes and weep, almost as if it were painful? I could not bear any more revelation. No other natural beauty that I had found in the other countries I have visited ever did this to me. Would I have the same reaction in Switzerland if I had seen just pure wilderness? I doubt it. I think I was marveling at a well-planned and ordered work of art coming from men cooperating with God's creation. Also, God was preparing me for a different experience I was to have at our first meeting that evening, but first I want to relate another experience I had a few months ago when I was privileged to meet a special artist and view some prints of his works.

This meeting I believe was a divine appointment. The name of the artist I met is Bas; I do not even know his real name. During the course of our visit, he explained the philosophy behind his artwork. He said that he never had any formal art training but

God had told him one day to quit college and to start painting. He would instruct him how to paint. Bas did just that, and God did what he said he would. As a result, Bas has painted pictures that are truly inspirational. He travels all over the world studying different kinds of animals in their natural habitat and waits for a revelation from God about the essence of that animal he is to paint. He then takes photos, may even do some sketches, and takes numerous notes. He takes these treasures back to the studio and then seeks to put on canvas what he has experienced in the spirit. He is very meticulous in his work. Sometimes, it may take him months to finish one painting. The animals he paints are not just of photographic quality but much more. Then, he develops the natural setting surrounding the animal in a more artistic fashion, playing with the various themes and variations of the shape and essence of the animal studied. I wept when I saw his pictures—beauty pierced my soul.

About forty seasoned intercessors from different European countries attended our conference, as well as several from the United States and Israel. The moderator asked all those in attendance to stand up and give their testimony. There was such a sense of awe as one by one began to share the price they paid to get to where they are today. Some were former Nazis who received a powerful revelation of the Jewishness of Jesus, almost to the level of the Apostle Paul's revelation of Jesus. Others shared how they had been imprisoned for their faith. It wasn't so much what was said, but it was through whom the words came. Such a sense of the fragrance of God emanated through their contrite spirits. I was once again pierced by beauty, not the beauty of the work of man, but of the work of God. It was the beauty of the bride that has made herself ready. She radiated. I began to weep again, as the beauty observed was experienced almost like a pain that could not be increased. Somehow, God had taken these men and women who willingly yielded to the hand of God, molded and shaped them, pruning away their excess branches, and constructed a work of art out of their lives.

As I reflect on the lives of others who have suffered the most and have given God the glory in the midst of their pain, I am awed at the beauty, the sweet aroma coming from them. There is something glorious emanating from a person who honors God in the midst of suffering. That person is caught up with things eternal and no longer looks to this life for fulfillment. Earth becomes but a temporary resting place. Her focus is on things above, and she becomes like Narnia's wardrobe, a place where heaven touches earth for all to see and enter in. Such is the calling of the last day's church, the bride, who has made herself beautiful by adorning herself with eternal jewels and clothing. Are we willing to suffer to display such beauty?

A story about an old saint who was imprisoned in concentration camps because of his active witness displays such beauty. He suffered intensely at the hands of his torturers, but always, he maintained a heart of gratitude and worshipped God. He said that the sweetest worship he had ever experienced was right there in the prison cell using his chains as instruments of praise. Since being released several years ago, he has traveled near and far to find a worship like the worship he experienced in prison but has found none.

On one trip, he related a story of how one of the guards kept mocking his faith in a loving God. He repeatedly sneered at this poor man, asking him what kind of God would allow his follower to go through such suffering. Finally, after many days of torment, this saint got up on his feet and stretched out his arms in identification with his crucified and risen LORD. At once, his countenance changed, and he began to radiate the glory and beauty of Jesus. The guard fell on his face, overcome with fear. Trembling, he asked the saint what must he do to be like him, and he gave his heart to the LORD. Such is the power of suffering to transform a person—beauty from ashes! Rejoicing transforms our arrows of adversity into bouquets of delicious flowers and fruit for others to enjoy.

Suffering, when responded to with worship and thanksgiving (recognizing the hand of God in the situation) instead of complaining and hardening of one's heart, will produce a beauty of inner character that will pierce the soul of another. So take heart, my friend, and God, the master craftsman, will take your ashes and make something beautiful out of them. Be patient and wait. In due season, you will reap what has been sown in the midst of your brokenness. I took comfort, and still take comfort, in the thought that an infinite, all powerful, yet loving, good God is working in my life to conform me into the likeness of his Son. He can be trusted, and I am excited about the unveiling that will take place of this masterpiece of art—me. "Work away LORD—may the beauty you work in me, as I overcome this great loss by your grace, someday pierce the soul of another, so he or she will yield his or her losses into your hands."

Seeing His Kingdom

Again, the kingdom of heaven is like a merchant looking for fine pearls. When he found one of great value, he went away and sold everything he had and bought it.

Matthew 13:45–47

In times of great turmoil and pain, I often looked for a purpose to keep going on with my life. There had to be something worth living for sufficient to lift me above all the evil and suffering. I became like the merchant in the above scripture that was looking for fine pearls. When I began to see the worth of the kingdom of God it began to be easier to give up my "rights" to a happy life here. God taught me how to live in and from the kingdom here on earth. This became the pearl of great worth where I was willing to sell all and go for broke. In fact, Acts 14:22 says that we have to go through many hardships to enter into the kingdom of God. The following illustration from the natural shows us the magnitude of glory sufficient to make all this suffering here as nothing in comparison.

The NASA experts calculate how much fuel a rocket needs to break free from the earth's atmosphere—the gravitational pull—before launching the rocket. They take into consideration the ship's weight, the ship's physical dimensions and shape, and the duration of the trip. When the rocket ship is on the launch pad and the countdown is completed, it is not until there is enough "lift" from the combustion of fuel before they drop the connector cables and free the ship to take off.

This word picture gave me a glimpse of what kind of power is needed to get us free from this "worldly kingdom" in order to dwell in God's heavenly kingdom. I often ask how much passionate love for God (fuel) I need to say "no" to the pull (gravity) of worldly thinking, desires, and attachments in order to soar with him. The bigger the circumstance I find myself in, or the greater the nature of the temptation that I am fighting, becomes the force or law that has to be overcome by the law of the spirit of life. "An object at rest remains at rest until a sufficient force comes to act upon that object." Such is one of the laws of matter. We will stay in our state of pain, of "earth-bound-ness," unless a greater force comes and moves us from our entrenched position. The love of God is our only answer, our only hope.

As you can see by reading the previous chapters of this book, God first had to capture my heart with a greater revelation of his great love for me. Then, in experiencing his great love for me through identifying with the great suffering he was willing to endure for my sake, my heart became aflame with love for him. This, then, became my power to endure and to choose life by laying down my own life and will. The love of God will be our only energy to endure to the end. No temptation, trial, nor suffering could ever have the power to divert the enraptured heart from its ultimate goal of finally beholding the face of the one whom it so dearly loves.

> The kingdom is only promised to those who love Jesus. Choose now who and which kingdom you really desire. If you love him you will endure anything! "For love is stronger than death; jealousy is as relentless and unyielding as Sheol: the coals thereof are coals of fire which hath a most vehement flame. Many waters cannot quench love, neither can the floods drown it" (Song of Solomon 8:6–7).
>
> *To Enjoy Him Forever* by Malcolm Webber, 79

I came to see that life is but a vapor and what happens to me here prepares me for my role in eternity. As I began to press into God with all my heart in the midst of my pain, he began to reveal the meaning of the kingdom. Many have asked how I made it through so much tragedy, and my answer sometimes is not satisfying because there is no formula. How does a person who is drowning get rescued? A person who believes he is drowning, where death seems a breath away, cries out for a rescuer. Then, the rescuer waits for the swimmer to spend his strength before he rescues him. I endured the pain of much change and loss during the years following Samuel's death. I was like a swimmer who was drowning and going down for her last breath. And God always brought relief by releasing more grace so I could endure; sometimes he even removed the pain completely.

As a result of his faithfulness, he ignited my heart with a deeper passion for his purposes concerning the kingdom of heaven. It was as if, within a few months (and years), the ropes that held me to this world were cut; God set me free to worship him in an even fuller dimension. Through his grace, he opened my eyes to see that this place was not my home. I came to see that life is but a vapor and what happens to me here prepares me for my role in eternity. He showed me that the level of my attachments here to family, friends, homes, and possessions determines the intensity of grief I experience when I am asked to give them up, either before the event of loss or after the event. My love for God had to be greater than my attachment to Samuel, my husband, my mother, my home, my physical health and comfort, my congregation, and my children. As the Scriptures say:

> Anyone who loves his father or mother more than me is not worthy of me; anyone who loves his son or daughter more than me is not worthy of me; and anyone who does not take his cross and follow me is not worthy of me. Whoever finds his life will lose it, and whoever loses his life for my sake will find it.
>
> Matthew 10:37–39

If we are not kingdom-minded, then the losses of this life will undo us. Daily I had to set my mind on things above, on his kingdom. Time and time again, we are admonished through the Word not to consider this place as our home. We are strangers and aliens here, citizens of the heavenly kingdom. We have to model our lives after the men and women written about in Hebrews 11 who were considered to be great people of faith.

Abraham, for example, made his home in the promised land, like a stranger in a foreign country. He lived in tents—temporary dwelling places. He looked forward to the city whose architect and builder was God. Because of his eternal perspective, he had the faith and courage to offer up his son Isaac. He knew that this life was not all that there was—this life was not the end or goal.

Abraham's example was very special to my husband during his grief process. It was really necessary for Dan to believe our son's death had meaning and purpose. He began to see Sam's death as a sacrifice. Whether or not it was a sacrifice given to the LORD that would bring great good was, as he saw it, to a significant extent a matter of the response of our grieving. By releasing Sam to the LORD and praising God in the midst of the anguish and tragedy, Dan felt that we became like Abraham sacrificing Isaac. Even though the "offering" was after the fact, my husband realized every such tragedy released something of the redemptive purpose and power of martyrdom when there was a faith response in the grieving. Martyrdom is a sacrifice of intercession that releases awesome power for the progress of the kingdom. It has been said that the blood of the martyrs was the seed of the church. Consequently, Dan was encouraged to see our loss as a sacrifice that would bring great good to the church and for the kingdom. Meaning and purpose became triumphant over tragedy; absurdity was defeated. For in our tragic loss, many across the world began to travail for not only the life of our son but for the restoration of Israel. People saw a connection between Samuel's restoration with the restoration of God's people, for the Messianic Jewish movement worldwide, and for the right relationship of Israel and the church. That's kingdom!

Other men of faith in the Bible admitted they were aliens and strangers on earth—people looking for a country not their own, a better country, a heavenly one which is the home of righteousness. Time and time again, we are admonished through the Word not to consider this place as our home. We are strangers and aliens here, citizens of the heavenly kingdom. Whenever we seek an earthly kingdom, we fall short of entering the "real" kingdom, which is spiritual and not carnal.

Since you call on a Father who judges each man's work impartially, live your lives as strangers here in reverent fear.

1 Peter 1:17

Dear friends, I urge you, as aliens and strangers in the world, to abstain from sinful desires, which war against your soul.

1 Peter 2:11

True worship happens when our minds are free from worldly attachments and self-concern. What will it take for our eyes to be opened to "see" and believe in the kingdom of heaven to the point when we can say like the Apostle Paul: "May I never boast except in the cross of our LORD Jesus Christ, through which the world has been crucified to me, and I to the world" (Galatians 6:14)? Have we discovered the pearl of great price, and are we willing to sell all that we have to obtain it? Or are we like the rich young ruler whose attachments to this world hindered him from coming into the kingdom of heaven?

The church is close to being powerless in America because this world has become our home. No wonder God adamantly states in his word that to be a friend of the world is to be an enemy of his (James 4:4–5). "Do not love this world or anything in the world. If anyone loves the world, the love of the Father is not in him" (1 John 2:15).

Hear God's heart. He is not trying to keep something good from us but has made a way so that we might have life—his life operating in us and through us. The kingdom of God is within us, and when we enter a room, we can say, "The kingdom of God is at hand." Greater works than what Jesus did we will do, but we must seek first his kingdom. His kingdom is manifest when his will is in manifestation in our hearts. If we understand the message concerning the kingdom, we will produce a crop a hundred-fold. We must die (to self and to this world) and value the eternal above the temporal.

Losing Samuel radically intensified my heart's cry, "May your kingdom come, may your will be done on earth as it is in Heaven."

I know that if I did not have this paradigm shift, I would not have made it through all the shaking in my life these past few years. All honor and glory goes to God for opening my eyes... I once was blind, but now I see. There is a greater gravitation toward heaven now, and Sam has become less "dead" to me. I am seated with Messiah in heavenly places. The LORD has been pleased to reveal his Son in me, and now I understand that the kingdom of God is about the glorification of his Son.

The message we are to preach is about Jesus and his kingdom! Suffering opened my eyes to see the kingdom, a kingdom where the river of life flows and brings to life everything it touches. When I saw from a kingdom viewpoint, I learned to see "death" for what it was and is. I saw that we are here on this earth to fight death until the day we enter into our heavenly home.

Life Triumphant Over Death

When the perishable has been clothed with the imperishable, and the mortal with immortality, then the saying that is written will come true: "Where, O death, is your victory? Where, O death, is your sting?"

1 Corinthians 15:54–55

More than any other experience, the loss of Samuel put me in touch with God's attitude toward death. When we left the graveyard that Friday afternoon and climbed into the black limousine, the stark realization finally hit—Samuel was not going to be returned to us in this life. His body was dead and buried.

People experience grief in different ways, but for me it was as if there was a weight pressing me into the grave with my son. I so much wanted to lie down next to him. Having a loving husband, children that needed me, and friends that loved me did not matter at that moment. I did not bless God for the other "fingers" that did not hurt—all I could think about was that "thumb" that was smashed with a hammer, radiating a pain so intense that I would do anything to escape.

Grief suffocates and paralyzes. I found myself in a daily battle against death. I had to birth the will to live and to believe in a loving God. Like never before Satan was tormenting me with thoughts of blame (it was somehow my fault Sam died) and unbelief in God's love and goodness. What was I fighting? I was fighting the spirit of death seeking to snuff out the life of God in my spirit. If Satan could get me to turn my back against God, then he would have won. The battle really became a battle between God and Satan over my heart.

I came to hate death with an intense passion. I was all too familiar with its stench and began to hate sin that brought death—not just physical death, but spiritual death. Both kinds of death bring the pain of grief because it is love that is grieved in the presence of death. Without love, there is no grief. I asked myself, "Do I stop loving to stop the agony?" How can I? It would then be joining the enemy who took Samuel's life.

All the pain and suffering in the world comes down to reaping the wages of corporate and individual sin. There is no escape. God wants us to have life… and more life… eternal life. Eternal life became the issue in the garden of Eden when Satan deceived Eve. Eating of the tree of life represented man's participating in God's all-powerful, creative, loving, thriving life—being one with him. Eating from the tree of the knowledge of good and evil represented a breaking from that life, from that oneness, and becoming independent, which brings a separation from the true source of life.

In the garden of Eden, God already had in mind eternal life for man as seen in the presence of the tree of life. This eternal life was to be according to God's mind and not man's mind. "The great thing in view for Adam was eternal life in a living fellowship with God. Satan struck a blow at that state in order to thwart that life, and he succeeded for the time being. Adam lost it through sin. Adam and Eve were then forbidden to eat of the tree of life lest they eat of it and live forever in their sinful state" (*Battle for Life* by T. Austin Sparks, 31). Man living apart from connection to the life of God dies, first spiritually and then physically. The spirit of Adam died in that he became separated from fellowship with God. So powerful was God's life resident in his mortal body that future generations inherited its vitality. It took almost two thousand years, or until the time of Abraham, for the life to wane from over nine hundred years to less than one hundred years. However, I marvel at how strong death is now because even though life or the spirit of holiness—resurrection power—permeated the mortal bodies of believers for almost two thousand years, man still hasn't been able to prolong his life. Only a few live to be one hundred years old! But one day, the dead will be raised to life everlasting, and we will receive bodies that will live forever. Yet when I was sitting at the bedside of my dying mother, I observed the mystery of life swallowing up death. What appeared to the natural eye as disease and destruction swallowing up the life in my mother's mortal body was seen as her spirit taking on immortality. It was as if I saw her becoming clothed in her new glory garments. The ugliness of decaying flesh began to glow with the beauty of eternity.

The last enemy to be defeated is death, so Satan is in a frenzy because he knows his time is short. In every way possible, he is seeking to rob, steal, and destroy... to swallow up life—God's life in his people. We have to see the battle as coming down to the battle over life. Don't we see it today, that one of the major battles being fought is over the issue of life—pro-choice versus pro-life? The proponents of pro-choice draw the battle lines as if choosing life had the same value as choosing death. Moral values are on the same level as one's preference for chocolate cake as opposed to yellow cake. How far we have fallen to believe that death is to be preferred over life! Any fruit that does not come from the tree of life produces death. Hear the heart of God as he pleads with his people Israel:

> See, I set before you today life and prosperity, death and destruction. For I command you today to love the LORD your God, to walk in his ways, and to keep his commands, decrees and laws; then you will live and increase, and the LORD your God will bless you in the land you are entering to possess. But if your heart turns away and you are not obedient, and if you are drawn away to bow down to other gods and worship them, I declare to you this day that you will certainly be destroyed. You will not live long in the land you are crossing the Jordan to enter and possess. This day I call heaven and earth as witnesses against you that I have set before you life and death, blessings and curses. Now choose life, so that you and your children may live and that you may love the LORD your God, listen to his voice, and hold fast to him. For the LORD is your life, and he will give you many years in the land he swore to give to your fathers, Abraham, Isaac, and Jacob.
>
> Deuteronomy 30:15–20

The laws he instated were for the purpose of empowering his people to live and not die. He is the one who made us, and he knows what will bring life and what will equip us for fruitfulness and blessing. Choose life, he pleads, that we may live and not die—that we might have the strength to go in and possess the land.

When Jesus came to earth, the cry of his heart was that we might have life and might have it more abundantly. He was called the "Bread of Life," "the Living Water," and "The Tree of Life." Out of his mouth came words of life. He was the Word become flesh. He was the life, the light that lighted up the world. All during his ministry, he demonstrated the way to receive that life. "I only do what I see my father doing. My will is to do the will of my father in heaven." He came as a light to the world, and that light was the life of man. Eternal life is to know God, to know what his heart is passionate over—that passion is for life, his life in us that we might be partakers of his glory. Abide in the vine, have his words abide in us, so that we might bear fruit, the evidence of a thriving life.

That life is maintained through obedience to his commandments, the greatest being to love God with all our hearts and to love our neighbor as ourselves. Do we value his life? Are we willing to fight for it, live it, and lay down our lives for it? If we do not passionately take up God's burden, then we will delay the day he puts death under his feet. We can be complacent no longer. The surge of hatred toward the life of God is increasing in the world. Soon the nations will rise up in rage against the people of God and will unite under one purpose, to destroy the life of God in his people. They want to stop the rule of God. Have you noticed the strong emotion behind the gay rights movement and the pro-choice movement? Their followers rise up in a boiling rage and even attack and mock the faith and beliefs of Jesus's followers. They passionately hate anyone who seeks to put forth an opposing view to their sinful lifestyle. Why is it that no one takes the name of Mohammed or Buddha in vain like they use Jesus's name? Do you ever hear someone say, "Oh Mohammed!"? In a New York art museum now they are exhibiting works that defame the Judeo-Christian faith; just see what kind of reaction there would be if they put up art defaming Mohammed or Buddha? Hear the words of Mike Bickle concerning this:

> Satan doesn't intend his perversion of human hearts to stop with the tremendous influx of indecency and immorality gripping the nations. He wants to push this thing way past mere immorality and indecency. His goal is for the nations of this earth to erupt with boiling rage against God. He is after militant, unified, passionate revolt against God's laws and even his right to reign ... Pockets of anger and rebellion are smoldering among those who influence and determine the general course of morality. Satan and his cohorts are fanning and feeding those flames so they will explode in rage and reckless revolt ... They plot to erase the wise boundaries of right and wrong, good and evil that God has marked out in his word for the human soul.
>
> *Passion for Jesus* by Mike Bickle, 74

No sooner does life get birthed into this world than Satan, the dragon, seeks to devour it. Cain killed Abel, Joseph's brothers tried to kill him, Pharaoh's army tried to kill the Israelites, and the Jewish religious leaders and the Romans (really all mankind) tried to put Jesus to death. The Nazis and numerous other people-groups tried to put to death the Jews. Why? Satan knows that when the Jews come to life (that is, come to the life found in Jesus), it would lead to the return of the LORD. That which is born of the flesh is always trying to destroy that which is born of the spirit. But the good news is that God's life will triumph—and has triumphed—over death.

I believe, that before the return of the LORD, his light (life) will burn so brightly in the lives of his followers that, though many will rage against them, many will turn from their wickedness. The Bible says that "the gospel of the kingdom will be preached in the whole world as a testimony to all nations, and then the end will come" (Matthew 24:14). It is the testimony of a resurrected life operating in the life of a believer ... not just the preaching of the good news of the gospel. We are to be the Word made flesh for all to read.

This is our inheritance. Let us be careful not to sell our birth-right for a pot of porridge, as did Esau, and then not be able to get it back though we cry for it with all our heart. Now is the time, in the midst of any pain and grief you might be suffering, to start embracing life again. There is a lot more at stake in the midst of your trial than just the loss of someone or something you love. The testimony of the life of God is at stake. It must triumph! This is our Goliath, the spirit of death, which is up in our face mocking the living God. You must not see just a huge mountain of grief coming against you but see the powers of darkness mocking and defying the living God. Do not let Satan land on the tails of your sorrow to defeat you! To love God means to love what he loves and to hate what he hates. Experiencing this tragic loss has so tied me into the heart of God that I have become like the burning bush. My campaign for life burns within me like a roaring fire, yet I am not consumed.

It is the efficacy of Jesus's resurrection life that is at stake when I allow myself to go into depression, bitterness, or allow my heart to become hardened. Has Jesus died for nothing? My one desire now has become that Jesus live his life through me—it is his testimony. He is the way, the truth, and the life.

When we come to realize that every time we go to the cross his resurrection life is released, then maybe we will be more motivated. Death will be at work in us (the death to self—separation from the old man) so that his life might flow through us to others.

> We always carry around in our body the death of Jesus, so that the life of Jesus may also be revealed in our body. For we who are alive are always being given over to death for Jesus' sake, so that his life may be revealed in our mortal body. So then, death is at work in us, but life is at work in you.
>
> 2 Corinthians 4:10–12

This powerful life is released as we practice being living martyrs; we present our bodies as living sacrifices. Every time we forgive, every time we give up our right to be right, every time we sacrificially love another, every time we say no to the lusts of the flesh, every time we say no to our will, every time we obey, his life is released. There will be more of him, less of me.

One way to put to death this flesh-life is through the combination of praying and fasting. When done under the unction of the spirit, it puts to death our flesh-life so that his life might be released. The instruments of darkness have learned this principle in reverse. The more they "meditate" and fast, the more death they release into the world. God help us in this battle against the spirit of death. The ultimate sacrifice is when we offer up our bodies as martyrs (when called upon by God.) One only has to look at history to see the power of life that was released following the murder of a saint. Often, whole cities or tribes would come to faith as the result of one man's or one woman's death. Look at what happened at the martyrdom of Stephen in Scripture… many came to faith. Revelation 6:9–11 mentions the souls of those who have been slain asking God how long before the end will come.

The end of this age will come when a significant number of his saints go to the cross, either through their lives being lived as a sacrifice or through their death. I think we have to expand our view of who is a martyr. It is not just the testimony of the courage of one who is martyred that testifies to the glories of God, but the courage of those who are left behind. The bereaved one's testimony of continuing to serve God with all his or her heart releases life too. Their love for God proves greater than their love for their human relationships.

Many tribesmen came to faith as the result of Elizabeth Elliot's courage and faith in the face of great tragedy. She lost her husband when one of the natives from the jungle where they were stationed as missionaries, murdered him. Instead of retreating in self-pity, she went back to that jungle with her daughter and continued to minister God's love to the natives. As a result, many came to faith; it wasn't just the result of the spilt blood of her martyred husband. "God, grant us this kind of love that beats with your heartbeat."

God will raise up a large company of believers in these last days who will love not their own lives even unto death. Though it will look like all is lost as the beast is given power to war against the saints, Jesus, in the power of his resurrected life, will triumph. Death will no longer reign and will be thrown into the pit of hell for eternity. Remember—life triumphs in the end!

Weapons of Life

For though we live in the world, we do not wage war as the world does. The weapons we fight with are not the weapons of the world. On the contrary, they have divine power to demolish strongholds. We demolish arguments and every pretension that sets itself up against the knowledge of God, and we take captive every thought to make it obedient to Christ.

2 Corinthians 10:3–5

Any crisis or loss in our lives presents an opportunity of great magnitude for growth, either away from God or toward God. It is a battle for life where God can receive great glory by showing the principalities and powers the greatness of his love and grace toward us in the mighty working of his resurrection power in us. Knowing what is at stake helped me to endure the pain. Somehow, my suffering was working in me a greater weight of glory and obtaining glory for God beyond anything I could possibly comprehend. His love was shown to be stronger than death.

In the first few months following Sam's death, I was able to break through almost daily. If I could push through to embrace life, thereby releasing his resurrection life, then it showed that God had won; death had been swallowed up by victory, by *life*. Daily to me, it was the garden of Gethsemane where a battle like unto the LORD's was taking place. Would my love for God be powerful enough for me to embrace his cup that he had chosen for me to drink? At times, it felt like I was sweating drops of blood in this struggle of my will up against the will of my father. Those times when I was able to say by the grace of God, "Not my will, but yours," I broke through to victory. Each time I broke through, something more was birthed in me of the revelation of God's goodness and his love. As time progressed, God would allow me longer periods of time of wrestling before receiving the breakthrough. His life then came in and swallowed up the death, and intimacy was restored. During these times, I learned that the weapons of life are powerful in coming against the spirit of hopelessness and death.

The Cross Is a Powerful Weapon of Life

Since I fought so hard to see Samuel healed, I lost my confidence in my ability to use spiritual warfare. In times past, using God's Word as a sword, or using aggressive prayer to stand against the onslaught of the enemy, was part of my usual arsenal. However, I did not have the emotional strength to do this type of battle after Sam's death. Besides, fighting in this way tapped into past wounds of not seeing God's promises come to pass. However, God, in his mercy and grace, showed me other weapons that were effective. The cross, coming to the point of dying to my will, became life to me. Truly the cross became the power of salvation, a place where moment by moment I had to meet my God. It became a matter of life and death. In Jesus, I moved, lived, and had my being. When I could get to the cross and release my pain into God's hands, he released his life into me. The cross became the greatest weapon of life for me. Often, I would meditate on scripture about the cross or meditate on passages from books that talked about the cross. Within a short period of time, I felt the darkness lifting that had tried to come on me.

Hope Is a Powerful Weapon of Life

Hopeless situations had to be avoided. I had to learn how to provide a protective cocoon for myself in which to grieve. Just like a bone marrow transplant patient has to be isolated from contaminants, I felt compelled to keep contaminants away from me as the grief-work was being accomplished. For instance, I found counseling people who had chronic problems to be emotionally draining. I was in a weakened state as I confronted my inability to solve my own problems. Since I struggled for hope, I became overpowered by the despair of others. It would open me up to the spirit of hopelessness and then to hopeless grieving. You never want to experience hopeless grieving. I did twice, and it was enough to scare me into the arms of God permanently.

One time, I participated in a counseling session a few months after Sam's passing that became a "he said/she said" hopeless battle. This and another event wiped me out, and hopeless grief crushed me. I entered into a wailing that would scare the most stouthearted. It was dark and evil and brought me into a deep pit of despair—a strong temptation to curse God and die. Thus, we found how important it was during those early days to surround ourselves with people who were full of hope.

Worship Is a Powerful Weapon of Life

We found that playing worship music twenty-four hours a day helped to provide a safe place for grieving to take place—a shelter amidst the storm. One might not think it necessary to play music while we were gone from the house, but we experimented with it. We found that the times we kept the music off while we were gone caused us to be "hit" with a ton of grief as soon as we entered the house. Being surrounded by worship music enabled us to grieve so it would not crush us. The worship music also penetrated our spirits so that when we had to leave the house, our spirits kept on worshipping. Often, I would listen to my spirit singing praises to God. Through worshipping, my eyes were opened to the realities of heavenly values and purposes. My heart became in tune with God's heart, and I became empowered to let go of my losses. Worship enabled me to receive comfort through the Holy Spirit—it was God's operating table.

In June of 2000, while Dan and I were in Israel, I dreamed that there was a major battle going on outside our house. It was as if spiritual forces were trying to knock our house down. I knew I had to go outside and face these demonic creatures that were trying to undo us. When I stepped outside our door, grotesque, ghost-like horses with wings swooped down upon my head. They kept biting me in an attempt to kill me. I kept trying desperately to fight them off, and finally I was able to grab one by the neck. At first, I tried using my physical strength to choke it, and then I tried a sword. Eventually, I tried rebuking it in the name of Jesus. The horse then changed into a creature that was clearly demonic, and it began to mock me, saying, "I am the demon that took Samuel's life." This enraged me, and I fought all the harder. Just when I thought I was a goner, I heard the voice of the LORD speak to me, "Patty, step away from him and no longer fight. I want you to focus on me and just worship." As I worshipped, the demon could not get near me. Every time he tried, he was blocked by some invisible field. And then, as my worship intensified, he began to shrivel up and die. Worship indeed proved to be a powerful weapon.

Praying in Tongues Is a Powerful Weapon of Life

I thank God for the years I have sown life into my spirit through regular times with him in the Word, in prayer, and in meditation. This built a "reservoir" of life, so when the drought came my leaves remained green. For months, I felt my spirit praying in tongues, even when I wasn't always consciously speaking to myself. It was like the Holy Spirit in my spirit was "taking over" and was strengthening my inner man so it could fight off death. It became evident that praying in tongues is a powerful weapon of life. We are exhorted in Scripture to pray in tongues regularly because it edifies us. It strengthens our inner man.

Positive Activities Are a Powerful Weapon of Life

We also found out that we had to avoid "escape-type" activities that deadened the process of grieving. This was mentioned earlier on in this book. Such things as video games and movies temporarily got our minds off the grief, but when the activity stopped, we experienced grief crashing in on us to the point where it was unbearable. This especially occurred after watching a movie with sensuality, too much violence, or bad language. It seemed like we became overly sensitive to those activities that did not add life to us. We could not afford any activity that did not build up our inner man. This is why I tried to use as many as these spiritual weapons as possible to sustain me.

Fellowship of Mature Believers Is a Powerful Weapon of Life

Another circumstance we found difficult to handle was being around crowds of people in the early stages of our grief. It became too overwhelming, yet we found being with a few close friends to be very uplifting. Being alone a lot may seem healthy and appropriate, but in the long run I think you will find your inner strength weakening. Your ability to grieve properly will be hindered, and the healing from the loss will be prolonged. Almost weekly, I would force myself to invite someone to lunch with me. Our conversations were not just around my pain, but I sought to find out about what was going on in my friend's life. We were also fortunate to have our two grown children living with us as well as three to four boarders during the hardest months of grieving. Our house was rarely without someone to talk to or to hug. This helped tremendously in fighting against the tendency to isolate myself in times of pain and sorrow.

Enjoying God's Creation Is a Powerful Weapon of Life

All during the summer following the accident and into the fall, my husband and I found healing as we sat on our deck in the morning. We would sit in our lawn chairs with our feet up, our cup of tea, our uplifting books, our Bible, and spend hours seeking the Lord. Soothing worship music played in the background along with the sound of birds chirping from the treetops. The sight of flowers in my garden added to the ambience of the setting. We had such a beautiful view from our deck. There was no need to go elsewhere to find the tranquility that can be found in God's creation. Truly drinking in the beauty of trees, grass, and flowers can promote healing to the nerves.

Doing Acts of Kindness Is a Powerful Weapon of Life

At one time during my grief-work, my heart became so over-stressed that I went to a heart specialist. I found out that my heart murmur had gotten worse and that there was a good chance I would need a valve transplant. I woke up during one of the medical procedures in which they had put an instrument down into my stomach to get a better echocardiogram of the heart. This so traumatized me that it sent me into a hopeless grief and a deep sense that God had betrayed my trust just like the doctors had betrayed my trust. This sent me on a downward spiral for a period of about two and one-half months. I have repeated the recounting of this incident here because of its relevance to what happened at my mother's house.

During this time, my mom, who was fighting the later stages of pancreatic cancer, took a turn for the worse and wasn't expected to live much longer. I had no choice but to go to my family home and attend to her needs before she died. I did not believe I would have the emotional strength to be with my mother as she died. In fear and trepidation, I went out of sheer obedience to what I believed God wanted. I had pretty much made up my mind that it was more than I could handle, and that everyone would understand if I did not show up; in fact, my father and brother and sisters had already released me from being with them and with my mother. They knew of the weakened state I was in. Through the power of his life in me, I somehow received the strength. In my estimation, I had nothing to give, but that nothing turned into a lot in the hands of God. I bathed her, emptied her bedpan, and did those things others thought too gross to do. Doing acts of kindness brought life to me! I couldn't read my Bible or pray, but I could play worship music and minister to my mom. Though I was fighting such fear and emptiness, God's arms were holding me tightly. I knew that where I was emotionally was okay and that I did not have to strive to break through. He was there. I had discovered the truth that doing acts of kindness is a weapon of life. Even making phone calls to cheer others up who were going through difficult times brought life to me.

Being Creative Is a Powerful Weapon of Life

Sometimes, you go through such a weakened period during your grieving process that you do not even have the strength to do the normal pressing in. That is why I have found these other ways to strengthen me when reading God's Word and praying was too much. Another weapon of life I found was doing something creative.

When I was attending my mom over Christmas vacation, I purchased some yarn to make afghans for our two children's upcoming weddings. For several weeks after my mom died, all I could do was cry, crochet, and listen to worship music. Those afghans became symbols of my grief-work and of my embracing life again. Crocheting was not a means of escape but a means of being fruitful in the midst of my fight against death. Therefore, being creative became a weapon of life for me.

Beauty Is a Powerful Weapon of Life

In the beginning, I felt compelled to add beauty to our home. I purchased new curtains in the living room, bought a new throw rug to cover some terrible "pet" spots on our gray rug, and obtained a nice entertainment cabinet to replace our old makeshift shelves. It seemed so important to surround myself with beauty. In choosing a temporary place to live until we could find a house to buy, I made it clear to God that I didn't care how big the place was, just that it would be beautiful. A few new, pretty clothes became important to me—even a nice piece of quality gold jewelry. I had to be careful not to make beauty an idol in my life, but I couldn't escape the fact that beauty was bringing healing to my soul.

I had gained a lot of weight during the years following Sam's death, so in 2002 I went on a strict diet to get back into shape. The good news is that I went down several dress sizes and had to buy a new wardrobe. Then, I discovered that shopping can act like a drug. In my quest for beauty, I went a little overboard. I finally understood how spending could be habit forming, especially when you are fighting depression.

Sports and Exercise Is a Powerful Weapon of Life

I would be remiss if I did not include some activities to which men (and some women) can really relate. My husband tells me that engaging in sports and exercise really releases built-up tension and aids in the healing process. He even tells me that watching sports is beneficial as the beauty of the execution of various plays and witnessing the skills of the players truly touches him deep within his soul. It gives him great joy and is a way for him to embrace life again.

Of course, it is a known fact that physical exertion restores the body to strength and health and even helps clear the mind. When we heal from grief we need to always take into account that our whole person—body, soul, and spirit—need to recover from trauma.

Dance Is a Powerful
Weapon of Life

Perhaps one of the greatest weapons of life I found was dance. The first time I gained victory through dance occurred the morning of the resurrection service. In preparing my heart for the difficulty I knew I would face, I put on an upbeat worship CD, and the spirit of worship overcame me. I began to dance out of gratefulness to a loving God. During the actual funeral service, I danced with victory before the LORD as an act of faith that death had been swallowed up by life. Having funerals where extensive mourning takes place is appropriate too, but we had sensed God wanted us to celebrate the life of Samuel, as well as the ultimate victory we have in Jesus. I felt and I do believe that great damage was done to the kingdom of darkness that day. Remember when I said that when something tragic happens Satan is up in your face spewing all sorts of negative words… well, when you start to dance, you get in a good upper cut, right to his face! He thought he got the victory, just like he thought he got the victory at the crucifixion of Jesus. But what he didn't count on, like then, was the power of resurrection life through the Holy Spirit!

The second instance occurred when Dan and I were in a particularly low state for several days. We had decided to go to Rock Church in Baltimore for one of their renewal services. All during the worship, I couldn't feel a thing. During Tommy Tenney's message, he spoke of the power of David's dance and his liberty before God. He admonished someone to step out in radical obedience and thereby release others into their freedom. He then called people forward who wanted prayer. Of course, Dan and I went forward. Tommy immediately made a beeline toward me, and I began to repent quickly of my self-pity and withdrawal. I told him that I would not give up the fight. He started rebuking the spirit of death off me and strongly urged me to choose life. He said that I could not afford to go down the road I was going and had to snap out of it. Immediately, something broke, and he asked me what happened. I told him something lifted off me and that I sensed God wanted me to dance like David did up on the stage. He told me to go for it. The spirit of the LORD came upon me, and I danced like a wild woman—did I ever feel liberty! The LORD swallowed up death that night! So much power was released that Dan fell over under the power of the spirit and was able to receive ministry too. Others broke free of bondages as well. Words cannot express the victory I experienced that night. I know damage was done to the kingdom of darkness again! So remember, dance, dance, dance, on the head of the enemy. The God of peace will soon crush Satan underneath your feet.

The third time where great victory was gained through dance was at my daughter's wedding in May of 1999. A close girlfriend of hers who was supposed to be part of her wedding party died the day of her dress rehearsal. The following day was the wedding. Was it possible to rejoice after such a loss? Yes, it is not a contradiction to experience joy in the midst of sorrow. In fact, it is very Jewish. During the reception there was such joy released as we began to do some of the traditional Jewish dances that are done at Messianic Jewish weddings. The grace of God was so evident as our community of friends joined with us to celebrate this joyous occasion. I danced and danced and cried and cried. I kept saying, "It feels so good to rejoice; it feels so good to rejoice." There settled over our gathering such a sweet sense of victory… the oil of gladness was given in the place of mourning. How blessed we all were that day! I surely wish you could have experienced that level of joy with us; it cannot be written in words. Somehow the joy was made richer because of the depth of the sorrow we had experienced together as the family of God.

Rejoicing Is a Powerful Weapon of Life

Along with dance is the weapon of rejoicing. Why do you think God continuously admonishes us to rejoice when we face various trials and hardships? Rejoicing brings God's power on the scene to fight the spirit of death that is trying to take us out in the midst of our pain and confusion. Rejoicing also is an act of faith that what we are going through will produce good fruit in our lives. Romans 5 and 1 Peter 1 say:

> Not only so, but we also rejoice in our sufferings, because we know that suffering produces perseverance; perseverance, character; and character, hope. And hope does not disappoint us, because God has poured out his love into our hearts by the Holy Spirit, whom he has given us.
>
> Romans 5:3–5

> In this you greatly rejoice, though now for a little while you may have to suffer grief in all kinds of trials. These have come so that your faith—of greater worth than gold, which perishes even though refined by fire—may be proved genuine and may result in praise, glory and honor when Jesus Christ is revealed.
>
> 1 Peter 1:6–7

Though we may not see the results of our endurance in the present, rejoicing is almost like a deposit guaranteeing that some day we will.

Living Here as a Pilgrim and Keeping the Mind-set of Eternity Is a Powerful Weapon of Life

Where I focused my thoughts played a very important part in regulating the intensity of my grief experience. We are admonished to focus on things above, on "whatever is true, whatever is noble, whatever is right, whatever is pure, whatever is lovely, whatever is admirable—if anything is excellent or praiseworthy—think about such things" (Philippians 4:8). If I spent too much time thinking about how much I missed Samuel, it brought me down. Not that it is wrong to think about the deceased one, but just that an overly morbid preoccupation with it can make for unnecessary pain. On the positive side, it is good to think about things eternal, about heaven, and about the love of the LORD. At first, it is very difficult to think about anything else but the tragic circumstances surrounding the death and the pain of the loss, but gradually you can train yourself to think about that which is still good about your life.

When death occurs, it is a reminder in the deepest sense of how temporary our life on earth is. We are but pilgrims passing through. Because of all the changes that had taken place in my life (the death of Samuel, the death of my mom, two children getting married, the move from a house we had lived in for ten years, two long-time boarders moving out, a best friend moving to Cyprus, and our resignation from the Beth Messiah pastorate after almost twenty-two years,) my attachments to this world have been ripped from me. According to the stress charts I should be a basket case, but actually, in January of 1999, I fell off the stress chart into the arms of the LORD. I feel totally free to do God's will now, as he has captured my heart so totally. I am a pilgrim looking forward to my eternal home where there is no more pain or sorrow, and I can eat freely from the tree of life once again. Think about eternity; think about the purposes of God for you to live and not die at this time, and think about the glory that will be yours and God's if you share in his sufferings.

These weapons I am describing to you do not require a lot of energy on your part. Grief-work is tiring, and the usual methods of warfare are too demanding of one's strength. Often, as I have said, using the Word as a weapon is difficult—at least it was for me. It was hard for me to concentrate. Also, doing aggressive spiritual warfare through prayer used too much energy. Basically, God did the battle for me. All I had to do was put myself in a position where his life was possible and welcomed. In each one of the activities I discussed above, it required very little inner strength, just a yielding to the ways of God in my life. Actually, they added strength instead of diminishing it. You will know instantly if the activity you are involved in brings a heavier grief so that you are unable to bear up under it. Conversely, you will know which activities bring a sense of lightness of burden, of greater inner strength, or of more grace to bear up under the load of grief.

God never intends for our grief to be more than we can bear, but we must be wise in how we choose to spend our time. I cannot stress this enough. Experiment if you do not believe me. I know these things I am sharing with you are true. Jesus came that we might have life and that life more abundantly. Yes, we can experience his life in the midst of the deepest pit, and he can raise us up to be overcomers.

All for His Glory

For our light and momentary troubles are achieving for us an eternal glory that far outweighs them all. So we fix our eyes not on what is seen, but on what is unseen. For what is seen is temporary, but what is unseen is eternal.

2 Corinthians 4:17–18

What's in it for me? How often this self-centered concern permeated my thoughts. If I had to go through this painful separation from Samuel, what benefit would I reap? Somehow, there had to be a "reward" for such suffering, otherwise, why endure? Though at first glance I appeared to be self-centered, God encouraged me through his word that there is some benefit to my submitting, and even rejoicing in my suffering—glory! What greater incentive can there be?

There is a purpose to suffering, even though we might hate it and seek to avoid it. Since the fall, death (disease, accident, sorrow, tears, etc.) has reigned; the wages of sin is always death. Death always separates us from the very life of God, his glory. Through man's self-assertion in the garden, death (separation) came into the world, but through the second Adam, Jesus, life and glory returned. Through his obedience unto death, eternal life returned as a possibility for man. In the same way, inherent now in the universe, is the law of the spirit of life that overcomes the law of sin and death. That law of life is the law of self-denial, of taking up our cross, and of losing our lives. When we come to the end of our lives, his life can then be made manifest in this world. His glory is the main purpose of our suffering.

Man was created for glory, but through seeking a glory of his own, he has ultimately received shame in its place. Adam and Eve hid from God in the garden as they were ashamed of their nakedness; glory was no longer their covering. Ever since, man has continued to make choices that has increased his shame, as any attempt to gain recognition through a "look what I have done" attitude cannot deliver a glory that will never fade. They exchanged the glory of the immortal God for earthly pleasures and achievements, and they worshipped and served created things (Roman 1:23, 25).

During one particularly painful week of grieving, I was connected by God with his heart of grief over his glory being removed. He took me through 2 Chronicles and certain passages in 1 Samuel and Ezekiel. I ended up weeping with him over his decision to remove the glory from his temple... from his people. Every time the Israelites departed from following God, the temple of the LORD was desecrated, and eventually his glory was removed. It was the testimony of God on earth, his presence, which became the issue. How he longs to have his glory fill the whole earth as the waters cover the beds of the sea.

At the end of Ezekiel we read of his glory returning to the future temple, perhaps to his living temple, the church. Haggai prophesied that the glory of the latter temple would surpass the glory of the former temple. I can't wait! Can you hear his heart's concern over his glory being made manifest to us? Jesus had the same concern for glory as his father.

> Father, the time has come. Glorify your Son, that your Son may glorify you... I have brought you glory on earth by completing the work you gave me to do... And now, Father, glorify me in your presence with the glory I had with you before the world began. All I have is yours, and all you have is mine. And glory has come to me through them. I have given them the glory that you gave me, that they may be one as we are one: "Father, I want those you have given me to be with me where I am, and to see my glory, the glory you have given me because you loved me before the creation of the world."
>
> John 17:1, 4, 5, 10, 22, 24

> The hour has come for the Son of Man to be glorified. I tell you the truth, unless a kernel of wheat falls to the ground and dies, it remains only a single seed. But if it dies, it produces many seeds. The man who loves his life will lose it, while the man who hates his life in this world will keep it for eternal life.
>
> John 12:23–25

Desiring glory—that is, the glory of God—is good and not bad. It gives God glory to fill us with his glory. Our momentary troubles cannot be compared with the weight of glory that will be revealed in us. If this scripture is to be a motivation for us to endure, we have to get a revelation of what that glory is and what it means to the heart of God.

The glory of God speaks of his inherent beauty, and his power, greatness, renown, and moral perfection... his very life. It is manifested in his perfect love toward us. Whatever God is pleased with he glorifies through his presence because the holiness of his being is satisfied. He wants to be known; everything he does has the ultimate purpose of bringing the whole earth to the knowledge of God. When we truly know him, our response is "Glory!"

God knows that the only way we can be recipients of that glory is to glorify him (acknowledge him) in all circumstances. Suffering of all kinds has the potential for bringing us to the end of our own self-effort (making us weak) so that God might come through in his mercy and grace to empower us. In this way, God is glorified—he gets the credit. The life of his son through the spirit is then magnified, and others give glory to God. We are always being given over to death so that his resurrection power may be made known to us, to others, and to the cloud of witnesses made up of saints and heavenly hosts. It is always not by our own might, or wisdom, but by the power of the spirit. This life is about God's work... not our own achievements after the flesh.

He alone is life. There is no life apart from him. He wants us to glorify him not because he is egotistical but because he knows that we will receive more life when we do. By acknowledging that he is the source of all life, we bring him glory and receive his glory in return.

We are predestined to be conformed to the image of his son. All suffering works in us this glory. We are being transformed from one degree of glory to the next. Knowing this, we can endure and learn to submit to the hand of God in our lives.

Perhaps the greatest character quality of Jesus that is formed in us through long suffering is meekness. Meekness in the Old Testament comes from the Hebrew word *anaw*, which means "suffering," "oppressed," "afflicted," denoting the character quality that is produced under such circumstances. It is that temper of spirit that accepts God's dealings with us as good, and therefore not something to be disputed or rebelled against. The humble man does not fight against God or contend with him in the face of injustices such as disease, accidents, or being sinned against by evil men (being falsely accused, slandered). When Jesus was insulted, he did not retaliate. We are to walk in his footsteps.

> Come unto me, all ye that labor and are heavy laden, and I will give you rest. Take my yoke upon you, and learn of me; for I am meek and lowly in heart: and ye shall find rest unto your souls.
>
> Matthew 11:28–29 (KJV)

> To this you were called, because Christ suffered for you, leaving you an example, that you should follow in his steps. "He committed no sin, and no deceit was found in his mouth." When they hurled their insults at him, he did not retaliate; when he suffered, he made no threats. Instead, he entrusted himself to him who judges justly.
>
> 1 Peter 2:21–23

So what is so great about meekness? Jesus said that the meek would inherit the earth. Also, Moses was the meekest man on earth and could be trusted with communicating with God face to face. I want that. Don't you? Meekness presents a formidable defense against Satan because it is the opposite of pride. Satan has nothing in which to gain a foothold in a meek person.

> Pride—to have everything in himself, to be as God, to be himself the seat of knowledge... Wherever there is pride, Satan has the ground that he wants for destroying and wrecking, and the risen LORD is providing ground against that by this tremendous object-lesson as to meekness. Yes, Satan, sinister, powerful and terrible as he is, can often be completely nullified by a spirit of meekness, his

> whole ground can be taken from him by a spirit of meekness… it destroys the very ground of Satan's authority.
>
> *We Beheld His Glory* by T. Austin Sparks, 136

This has been a hard lesson for me to learn. How often I have fought against having to go through this whole grieving process and have even become angry. I wanted answers and experienced much turmoil over God's apparent silence. Then he taught me about meekness.

Another great purpose of God attained through suffering is the provision of a bride for his son… an eternal companion.

> If God was to realize his purpose in creation, to obtain an eternal companion for his son, he had to suffer. It was unavoidable. If the bride was to be qualified to rule with him, she also had to suffer. This illuminates the passage in 2 Timothy 2:12, "If we suffer, we shall also reign with him."
>
> *Don't Waste Your Sorrows* by Paul Billheimer, 21

As his eternal companion, we must learn how to love as he loves and learn how to suffer as he suffered. That means we have to learn agape love—the love that suffers for another because it lays down its life for the other. "There is no love without self-giving. There is no self-giving without pain" (Billheimer, 36). All suffering, if received with the right heart, works toward our decentralization. There is no such thing as a saint that has not suffered. Though we always seek healing or deliverance, and sometimes we triumph by receiving these promises, yet if the symptoms persist we learn a new dimension of agape love. Our eternal rank is then increased. Paul Billheimer puts these truths to print in such an excellent way. I wish I could reprint his whole book here, but since I cannot, I would suggest that you purchase your own copy and read it for yourself. This book brought me great comfort this past year.

> Suffering, from whatever source, of whatever nature, and of whatever intensity, plus triumphant acceptance equals character… Affliction, triumphantly accepted here, means rank there because

this is the way God builds selfless character and develops agape love. Suffering, triumphantly accepted, slays the self-life, delivers one from self-centeredness, and frees one to love.

Billheimer, 50–51

The center of gravity of God's discipline is not time but eternity. Allowing God's discipline to wean one from vain ambition and selfishness increases agape love and transmutes one's brokenness into eternal glory. Rejecting and refusing the painful circumstances we are in will work to waste our sorrows. There are times when our best response to suffering is to say *not my will but yours be done.* We can put our full trust in a loving God that will work toward our ultimate good as he has eternity in mind.

All the unspeakable suffering of the saints, the combined sorrows, tragedies, heartaches, disappointments, the persecutions and martyrdoms in the history of the Church Universal from the first century to this present throbbing moment, all of these can be justified only by taking eternity into consideration... Suffering is God's grand strategy for creating rank in the Bridehood for his eternal enterprise.

Billheimer, 81

Such suffering not only produces agape love in us, but it also weans us from our attachments to this world. As mentioned before in this book, through many changes over the years, I went through a crisis of value assessment. How much does this world really have to offer? What is most important in this life? What will give me the greatest reason to go on living?

Whenever anyone suffers intensely, questions are raised. Through the process of working through the issues, I often turn my heart toward heavenly values. A purification of the heart takes place, and nothing seems to matter but pleasing God. Throwing off the sin that so easily entangled became easier as I contemplated my purpose here and how short life is. I no longer wanted to waste time beating the air. Heaven became my true home, and endurance became dependent on my continued heavenly focus. My heart had to be set on pilgrimage. I want all my energies to be channeled toward bringing glory to God. Otherwise, why live?

You see, suffering got "me" out of the way so I could see God. I came to know the power of his grace to sustain me. When I felt my foot was slipping, others prayed for more grace. I was then empowered to endure. I would not have known the power of his grace if I had not been tried sorely through the years and made weak in my own strength. It is a miracle that I am full of joy at the present moment. Paul's word about delighting in his weaknesses has found an agreement in my spirit. For it is when I am weak that he is strong. Malcolm Webber in his book *To Enjoy Him Forever*, beautifully explains this:

> As we turn our hearts fully toward God to obtain his strength in time of suffering, and do actually receive from him comfort and strength, we will accordingly have a store of spiritual comfort and power out of which we can give to others in their time of need… It is only when death is really working in us that the life of Jesus will flow out of us to others. We can only give to someone what we ourselves have first received. So it is clearly evident that without union with Christ (Messiah) in his sufferings, God can never use us for the fullest blessing of others.
>
> Webber, 131

God has greatly comforted me over the loss of Samuel, and he has opened up many doors where I could share with others the comfort I have received. Many have been encouraged and strengthened. I praise God for the life he is releasing through his testimony of grace in me.

Lastly, it is through suffering that we learn obedience. It is easy to obey when we are asked to do something that agrees with what we esteem as good and best. But when we are asked to do something that is disagreeable, suffering takes place. No one likes to experience conflict of interests and have to continually give up her own interest to serve another's. Jesus learned obedience through the things he suffered—"Although he was a son, he learned obedience from what he suffered" (Hebrews 5:8).

It is easy to love God when everything is going our way, but what happens when we find ourselves in a situation that is uncomfortable or painful? Loving God will eventually cost us everything we have and are.

Likewise, trusting God is easy when all our needs can be met through our own efforts. But how about when we are sick, or struggling financially, or suffering a great loss in our life? *It is only when we come up against something we cannot change that our faith really has a chance to develop.*

First Peter 1:6–7 tells of the importance of trials to refine our faith so that it will prove genuine and eventually bring glory and honor to God. It is only through the spiritual exercise of faith that we are strengthened and matured, as can be seen from the following quote by Webber.

> Muscles need resistance to grow strong. And it is only after it has begun to hurt that anything is being built. Dead wood beneath the earth needs great pressure to be transformed into coal which is useful. And with even more pressure diamonds can be formed. In the same way, our spiritual character must have opposition and resistance for it to mature. Pain must be experienced. Pressure must be endured. It is through overcoming temptation and trial that we grow spiritually strong. It is through suffering, in all its forms, that we have the opportunity to learn obedience to God and to be perfected by him. Thus our trials and sufferings mature us, making us perfect and complete before God, and partakers of his glory.
>
> Webber, 131

Many years have passed since the death of our son. How grateful I am that I have come through the valley of the shadow of death and am back in green pastures. During this time, God moved my family several times. A year after the fire we moved to a townhouse while we were on sabbatical. One day we were out for a drive, and we got temporarily lost along a lonely country road. We happened upon a property that had two houses for sale on it. It has been one of our son's dreams to live next to us, so this seemed like it might be something to look into. We ended up purchasing the place.

I wept with tears of gratitude the day we took up ownership. As I was sitting alone on our beautiful, large deck, I marveled at God's unfathomable ability to bring sorrow as well as blessing. This home became a place of healing for all of us. It was a beautiful ranch house situated on two and one-half acres of land in the country. Our backyard was filled with mature trees and had a small stream which forms the back border of our property. I called this house my Psalm 23 house for God had shepherded me back to wholeness there. I even planted a beautiful perennial garden as a memorial to Samuel's life. Working in this garden had been so therapeutic for me, and God had often spoken tender words to me in the midst of my pulling weeds. Gazing into all those beautiful flowers once again confirmed to me the power of beauty to heal.

After five years of living in our country house God made it clear that we had to sell it and move once again. Our travels, as well as our spending six months in Israel each year, made it impossible to keep the place up. Because we were able to sell the house at top value (it had more than doubled during the time we were living there) we were able to purchase a small condo in Florida and a house in Israel. It doesn't seem so long ago that I was sitting in my recliner, wondering if I were going to make it through another day. At that time, I felt like our work for God was over, but now I see that it has only begun. We are excited as we see God's plans keep unfolding for us.

Our dream to work with young, Jewish people in Israel, discipling them in character and leadership, and preparing them to be fruitful in the kingdom of God is being realized. We are so privileged to be able to have young people live with us and be able to be instruments in bringing them more and more into the image of the Messiah. Also, God has used us to help strengthen the other ministries in the land and use Israel as a base for traveling to Europe and Africa to minister in various venues. Truly our lot has fallen in pleasant places and he has indeed extended the "tent pegs" of our dwelling place.

As part of our travels, God has been using us to awaken the church to her Jewish roots and her responsibility to support and align herself with Israel. God is connecting us with some awesome believers who have suffered much for the gospel. It seems like God is networking many of his saints for his end-time purposes. Sometimes it feels like we are privileged to feast at his banqueting table and are enjoying the fellowship of the bride and bridegroom a little early.

Recently I was called back from Israel to take part in a judicial settlement concerning the fire. I was so excited to see the family in whose house the fire was. We had not seen each other for years and I knew that were still some unresolved issues on both of our sides. The three young men from that family were so happy to see me. They were so concerned about how I was and were carrying a load of guilt like I suspected. My heart went out to them and I was able to be like Joseph and tell them not to be too hard on themselves. It was not them that caused Samuel's death, ultimately, as God was in control. I reassured them that God has brought a lot of good from this tragedy and I hugged and released each one of them from the burden they were carrying. It was important for them to see that I had overcome and was walking in joy. How do I convey the exhilaration of my mother's heart as I saw weights leave their shoulders? Also, their mother observed what was going on and came over and hugged and hugged me. No words were necessary. I had one of my nagging questions answered that had repeatedly surfaced over the years. Was God's presence felt in the fire the same way I was experiencing his presence outside the house? Did Samuel suffer? These precious young men gave me an accounting of what happened and how they felt a supernatural presence and peace as they each passed out from the smoke. I was assured that the same thing happened to Samuel before he was burned.

I was also able to reassure the father that we had forgiven them and told him how much our family loved them. Indeed there was closure between our families, and we tasted a bit of heaven that day.

The goodness of the LORD in the lives of my family and myself already outweighs the sadness of this tragedy. One time, I asked two of my mother's close friends a question. Both of these women had lost two children and a husband, yet they went on with life and kept their faith in God. I asked them how they survived. They each responded, independently, that they chose what to think about. That was their answer to me, but at the time, this answer made me angry. I was still in raw grief, and I could not comprehend how I could choose not to think about my loss. But now I see that their answer was right. In time, I gained the grace to choose what to think about. I choose to reflect on the blessings God has brought out of our lives rather than focus on the pain of loss. I am rich, rich, rich, for behold, in his time he has made all things beautiful.

Suffering, unfortunately, has the power to destroy some while it perfects others. It is not the suffering itself that benefits us but our response to it that transforms us. By yielding to God in the midst of our trials, we allow the ministry of the Spirit to bring us from one degree of glory to the next. It is a progressive maturing and not a quick work. The process itself is valuable because it is the trip along the way that makes us weak and teaches us to rely upon God and not ourselves. We will always be on this journey called life. It is a gift from God; we only have a few short years to enjoy it. I look at my life now as God's medium out of which he is working to create a beautiful masterpiece. We are not like the other art media that are subject to the will of the artist but are living media. Somehow, in the interaction of our free will and God's sovereignty, this work of art is developed over the years. Our choices (both good and bad), circumstances, others' choices, and God's actions are being woven together and refined in the fires of mystery. At times, I get glimpses of what God is doing, and my heart becomes overwhelmed with gratefulness. Through the storms of life and the days of sunshine, he never stops molding and shaping my life. The sorrows as well as the joys go into this medium "life," and both experiences interplay off each other to form an exquisite work of art. Yes, I choose life. Life has triumphed! And all for his glory!

Appendix

Letters of Comfort from Samuel's Friends

Stephanie's Story

My hero was my good neighbor, Sammy Juster. I chose him as my hero because he was one of the two boys to die in a fire next door to me.

He was my boy best friend. When he passed away, I wasn't taking it too well.

He was brave because he would always want to stand up to older people and prove them wrong. He stood up for his sister when she was having a problem with some of the other neighborhood kids. Sammy was a caring person. He cared for his sister, his family, and his friends.

Sammy had a love for animals. When he was about nine years old, he found a baby bird that couldn't fly and had fallen out of its nest. While the baby bird was healing, he kept it in his home and would find worms and things for it to eat. After he had set the baby bird free, he found a hurt squirrel that he took into his home until it healed.

Sammy left behind his golden retriever named Butter. He would rollerblade while trying to walk Butter; instead Butter would love to run and pull Sammy behind her. Butter really misses him. My dog Rowdy and Butter have become really good friends since Sammy's death. I think this helps Butter to not be as lonely.

He was also very active. Sammy was one of the best baseball players I knew. He got my cousin into playing baseball when he would come and visit my house. He would take my cousin outside and show him how good he was at it. Soon, my cousin was also very good.

Sammy was different from me in a lot of ways but we were also very alike. Sammy was a Christian Jew, and I am Catholic. He liked music from his church, and I like pop music. The differences between us didn't matter. We were still friends.

The event that led Sammy to become my hero was his death. It had a major effect on me and changed my life. Through all the years I knew him, we had shared many things together. After his death, I will never be the same and can never share those good times with him again.

I miss him very much. May Samuel Juster rest in peace.

Another little girl wrote the following, which I have left unchanged:

Kelly's Story

1. Me first reson why sammy is my personal hero is for his citizenship. Sammy would cut people's grass and pull there weeds in the summer time. In the winter he would shovel people's snow.

2. Sammy also was a very caring person he carried about everyone's feelings even if he really didn't know you.

3. He was a very respectful person to his team mates, parents, brothers and sisters, friends and even people he didn't really know like when he first met me he really didn't know me but said hi anyway.

4. One thing he would never give in to people making fun of him. He really didn't bother with what they thought about him.

5. Sammy had always wanted a dog he would litterly beg his mom for a dog my main point here is he had a goal his goal was to get a dog he never gave up, in result he finally gets a dog and names it butter and he has to leave.

This third report is a literary piece from another neighborhood girl. This piece brought me to tears when I first read it a few months after Sam's death.

A Day without Sunshine, by Sarah

I sighed as I sat upon my roof with the warm July wind blowing through my hair. My parents would never let me up here, but since they weren't home I thought it was a good opportunity. I looked around our empty court and sighed again as I clutched my knees to my chest and rested my chin upon them. I kind of missed the fact that the kids in the neighborhood were gone, but I guessed it was just part of growing up. "People do get older," I thought to myself. No more toys scattered across the lawn, and there was no longer any hopscotch drawn on the streets in chalk. That was okay, though; it wasn't like I had an urge to hopscotch or anything.

It was Sammy whom I missed. We had grown up together, but he was gone now. I turned my head and looked at his house, then looked toward the window of his room; his parents had left it just the way it was. I thought about the long nights when all the kids would run around outside catching fire flies and longed to have those days back. Then I smiled slightly with the thought of the cold winters where it seemed as though the snow would never stop falling from the sky and we'd all go sledding all day. "Ah, those were good memories," I thought. My slight smile turned to a frown as I realized that there would be no new memories involving my friend. Sammy had died when he was only twelve.

I did not want to get myself all upset, so I put a smile back on my face and tried to enjoy the beautiful weather. As I sat there wondering what he would be doing now, a bird flew by and landed on the tree near the roof. "Hello, birdie," I said as it stared back at me. The bird flew off and I sighed once again. I looked down at my front lawn and again thought of all my happy childhood memories and thought about those wonderful days of sunshine. Oh no, I thought to myself, as the gentle breeze turned into a series of rough winds and clouds started to form above my head. I closed my eyes tight and thought of those days when we were all happy and the sun seemed to always be shining. Then, I opened my eyes and looked up at the sky to feel a raindrop hit my nose. Oh well, I guess I can handle one day without sunshine, I thought. I stood up from my crouched position and stretched as more and more rain began to fall from the sky and quickly went back through the window into the house. It was raining now, but I will always remember the sunshine.

These precious girls blessed me immensely. Parents have so little idea what kind of impact their children make on others, and such reports brought joy to my soul. I am so grateful to Yeshua for comforting me through the words of little children.

Endnotes

CHAPTER SIX:

The Sh'ma is a Hebrew prayer that is sung in the synagogue every Sabbath calling the Jewish person to faithfulness to one God. It is taken from Deuteronomy 6:4–5 and often includes verses 6–9 as well. The Aaronic Benediction is a Hebrew blessing spoken or sung over the congregants or individuals and is taken from Numbers 6:24-26.

CHAPTER SEVENTEEN:

This is a Jewish practice where friends of the bereaved family sit with them every day for a week, bringing them food and serving them. Also, they make a point to talk about the deceased one and avoid frivolous chatter. The family finds comfort as their friends enter into mourning with them.

Bibliography

The following books brought me a great deal of comfort during my year of grieving. Some of them I have read over several times. I strongly suggest you purchase and read them devotionally. May you be blessed as I have been in making these books my "friends."

Bickle, Mike. Passion for Jesus. Orlando: Creation House, 1993.

Biliheimer, Paul E. Don't Waste Your Sorrows. Minnesota: Bethany House Publishers, 1977.

Cowman, L.B. Streams in the Desert. Grand Rapids: Zondervan Publishing House, 1997.

Crabb, Larry. Finding God, Grand Rapids: Zondervan Publishing House, 1993.

Fry, Steve. A God Who Heals the Heart, Brentwood, Texas: Deep Fryed Books, 1997.

Nee, Watchman. The Release of the Spirit, Sure Foundation Publishers, 1965.

Sparks, T. Austin. His Great Love; Immanuel Church: Tulsa, Oklahoma (no copyright).

—Battle for Life; Tulsa: Immanuel Church (no copyright).

—Prophetic Ministry; Tulsa: Immanuel Church (no copyright).

—We Beheld His Glory, Tulsa: Immanuel Church (no copyright).

Webber, Malcolm. To Enjoy Him Forever, Kimmell, Indiana: Pioneer Books, 1990.